Magical Uses for Magnets

In memory of
Al H. Morrison, BA
astrologer, friend, and a
very magnetic man, indeed

Magical Uses for Magnets

Draja Mickaharic

Ibis Press
An Imprint of Nicolas-Hays
Berwick, Maine

First published in 2004 by
Ibis Press
An imprint of Nicolas-Hays, Inc.
P. O. Box 1126
Berwick, ME 03901-1126
www.nicolashays.com

Distributed to the trade by
Red Wheel/Weiser, LLC
P. O. Box 612
York Beach, ME 03910-0612
www.redwheelweiser.com

Library of Congress Cataloging-in-Publication Data available on
request.

VG
Cover and text design by Phillip Augusta.
Illustrations by Alden Cole.
Typeset in ITC New Baskerville. Display type: Mezz
Printed in the United States of America
10 09 08 07 06 05 04
7   6   5   4   3   2   1

The paper used in this publication meets the minimum require-
ments of the American National Standard for Information
Sciences—Permanence of Paper for Printed Library Materials
Z39.48–1992 (R1997).

Note to readers: This book is meant for informational purposes only. The author and publisher are not responsible for
the manner in which the material is used or for the results
obtained. Before using any technique for healing purposes,
always consult a medical professional.

Contents

Illustrations

Illustrations

Introduction

Magnets are one of the great unrecognized conveniences of modern life. From catches on our kitchen cabinets, useful tools in our workshops, and the magnetic strip on our credit and bankcards, magnets of all kinds play an important part in our daily life. It has not always been so, although fascination with the living stones—lodestones that drew bits of iron to themselves—has been noted by the curious since they were first discovered in remote antiquity.

Although there was probably some academic interest in these living stones expressed before the 12th century, there is little record of it aside from myths. In the 15th century and before, ground lodestones were used medicinally. At one time, ground magnets were used in an effort to cure the bubonic plague. (But almost everything else was also used as a medication at that time, always with dismal failure as the result.)

Because lodestones attracted small bits of iron to themselves, they became known as "living stones." From there it was but a short step to using them in folk magic, usually as an attracting influence. The later use of magnets in the practice of the magical arts was enhanced by the reputation of the promoter of the animal magnetism theory of life—Franz Friedrich Anton Mesmer, whose many successful cures were not enough to keep a royal French commission of inquiry from condemning his work.

Over the last 200 years, the occult or hidden uses of magnets have grown, along with their more worldly applications. In this book, I hope to give some idea of their hidden, or at least lesser known, uses. I hope that this will stimulate more research into magnets as useful tools in the everyday life of practicing occultists. I detail some of the subjects herein, while I have only touched upon others. There is plenty of room for an interested experimenter to elaborate on the information given in these pages.

You can make most of the devices I describe quite easily in your home workshop, with a minimum of mechanical or electrical skills. You may experiment with them and judge for yourself their usefulness. Experimentation with magnets may become a useful hobby, if nothing else!

—Draja Mickaharic

CHAPTER 1

A Bit of History

When and where the property of magnetism was first discovered will probably always be an unresolved matter for scholastic debate. The story of a Cretan shepherd named Magnes finding that the iron point of his staff was attracted to certain rocks in the ground of Mt. Ida is most certainly a myth. However, like many myths, it makes a good story, and it provides a simple explanation. A similar tale is that of a shepherd in the province of Magnesia in Asia Minor, now Turkey, who had the same experience while tending his sheep. The name of that ancient city-state has now become identified with all things dealing with magnetic forces.

Lodestones, natural magnets, are found in many places around the world. These natural magnets are often found wherever there is a mass of naturally-occurring iron ore in the form of an iron oxide, magnetite (Fe_3O_4). This heavy rock, usually black in color, is often crystalline, but sometimes it is just a massive black stone. Scientifically, lodestone is thought to be a form of magnetite that gained its magnetic properties by being struck by lightning. The lightning strike imparts a very brief, but very powerful electrical current that is accompanied by an equally powerful magnetic field. Some experiments By Dr. Peter Wasilewski at the Langmuir laboratory of the University of New Mexico have demonstrated that this theory of magnetism being induced in magnetite by a random lightning strike is quite probably correct.

There are other oxides of iron, not all of which are magnetic, or able to be magnetized. Red iron oxide, (FeO and FeO_2) is not drawn to the magnet at all. It seems that only magnetite is magnetized by lightning to become the lodestone.

From the time of the discovery of lodestones, probably by the Arcadians, Greeks, Chinese, or by all of them independently, until about the 19th century, the lodestone was the only available magnet. Lodestone charms inscribed with the symbol of the god Marduk have been found in ancient Sumer. From the time of its discovery, lodestones were almost certainly used in magical practices. Because of its unique property of attracting iron, many additional myths and stories gathered around this strange stone. As a result, lodestones soon became the source of many fanciful and wonderful stories. Archimedes (287–212 B.C.), in one fanciful story, was supposed to have drawn the iron nails from enemy ships, sinking them. Even today, using the more powerful electromagnets now available to us, that would be a difficult task to accomplish.

In about 70 B.C., Titus Lucretius Carus in *De Rerum Natura*,[1] said that a lodestone could support a chain of little iron rings, each adhering to the one above it. He did not recognize this as magnetic induction, but thought it only to be another natural curiosity of lodestones.

Pliny the Elder (A.D. 23–79) wrote that there was a hill near the river Indus that was made entirely of a stone that attracted iron. Myths of magnetic islands that attracted ships to them also circulated. There were many other marvelous and amazing stories concerning the lodestone, most of them without any foundation at all. In a romantic story dating to the middle of the 12th century, magnets were described as a municipal defense device. This story, the "Roman d'Eneas," written about 1157, gave a fanciful description of lodestones being placed in the wall of Carthage. The lodestones supposedly attracted and held fast men wearing iron armor. Thus, the lodestones in the walls protected the city from invasion.

Because of their seeming to be alive, through their property of attracting small bits of iron, lodestones soon gained both a mystical and a semi-scientific reputation. For many years, the effects of magnetism, and the lodestones that produced it, were only one of many natural curiosities in the world that puzzled and amused those who knew of them. Lodestones drew far less the interest of serious investigators than of romantic writers and storytellers.

The compass, which indicates direction by use of a magnet pointer, was apparently first mentioned in Chinese writings of about A.D. 83. There was a reference to a "south-pointing spoon" found in documents of that time. Chinese maps, like astrological charts, orient south at the top. In this, they are unlike American and European maps, which have north placed at the top. Therefore, the Chinese would navigate by the use of a south-pointing instrument, rather than one pointing north. Whether or not anyone ever connected the similarity of magnets and the pointing of the compasses before the 12th century is another matter for academic scholars to debate.

The Chinese apparently used their magnetic south-pointing indicators only for travel on land. A Chinese writer, however, mentions that "foreign sailors" used a magnetic compass on ships sailing between Canton and Sumatra. By the first decade of the 12th century, Chinese geomancers were using the magnetized needle compass. Today, the geomancer's compass is not a magnetic instrument at all, but rather an aid in calculation and orientation. The magnetic compass is only a supplement to the geomancer's compass, the instrument upon which the geomancer relies.

The earliest European mention of the compass was made by Alexander Neckham (1157–1217), a monk of St. Albans, England. In his work *De Naturis Rerum*,[2] he described the compass, but he did not seem to consider it a new invention. The compass apparently was first introduced to Europe sometime in the 12th century. By the first quarter of the 13th century, magnetic compasses were considered a navigational necessity. Early studies of magnetism, such as they might have been, were done for purely practical matters, primarily to further the development of the mariner's compass. The mariner's compass quickly developed into a more elaborate, and over time, a more accurate instrument. Meanwhile, ordinary people who traveled over land during the late Middle Ages used smaller lodestones suspended to move freely on strings.[3]

As with any other unknown, myths and strange tales abounded concerning both the mariner's compass and the magnetism of lodestones in general, although the similarity of the two was not very well connected at that time. Garlic was not allowed on some sailing ships, for fear that its fumes might influence the sensitive compass. Other superstitious prohibitions concerning the compass and sailing ships abounded. Columbus believed that the compass was attracted to the pole star, apparently making no connection between the compass and magnetism at all.

About 1236, William Auvergne, the Bishop of Paris, compared the motion of the celestial spheres to magnetic induction, the ability of a lodestone to magnetize a small piece of iron. He put forward this interesting theory in his book *De Universeo Creaturarum*. These celestial spheres were believed to move within each other, Earth being placed at the center.

The first more or less "scientific" mention of magnets was by Petrus Peregrinus de Maricourt, a French crusader. In 1269, he wrote to a countryman his *Epistula de Magnete* (*Letter on the Magnet*),[4] concerning lodestones. Petrus Peregrinus, according to Roger Bacon, was the greatest experimenter of his day. In his *Letter on the Magnet*, Peregrinus explained how to identify the poles of a magnet (which he named in the belief that they were somewhat like Earth's poles) and discussed their attraction and repulsion. His letters made the connection between the compass and natural magnets obvious. He also identified the lines of magnetic force, and discussed how magnetism may be transferred from lodestones to the needle of a compass. His *Letter on the Magnet* so completely covered the knowledge of magnets available at that time that it stood as the authoritative text on the subject of magnetism for the next three hundred years.

In his voyage to America in 1492, Christopher Columbus noted that the compass needle did not point exactly to the north, as indicated by the pole star. While in Spain, the needle veered off slightly to the east. As he sailed east, he claimed that there were slight changes in the direction in which the needle pointed, ending up with the compass needle pointing slightly west of north when he was in Haiti. In 1498, Columbus wrote his observations, suggesting that the error in the compass, pointing either east or west of true north, might depend on the location of the compass on the earth. This error is called the declination error, or the compass error. Columbus's finding was not widely accepted at the time, nor are all of his observations on the compass universally accepted today. However, once the compass error was noticed and accepted, it became of great importance to sailors to know just how far their compass needle was pointing away from true north.

Phillippus Aureolus Paracelsus (1493–1541), the well-known medical innovator, occultist, and alchemist, claimed that the magnet attracts all of the "martial humors" found in the human system. He went on to instruct that the magnet be placed in the center of the illness, to attract the illness to it, thus destroying the head of the virus and curing the patient. He especially recommended this treatment for inflammations, fluxes, ulceration, diseases of the bowels and uterus, and in both internal and external diseases.

In 1581, Robert Norman of London described in his book *The Newe Attractive,*[5] another interesting effect of the compass. If a compass needle was perfectly balanced before being magnetized, after it was magnetized, its north end would dip downward, and a bit of the tip had to be snipped off to restore the needle's balance. This indicated to him that the force on the compass needle was not horizontal, but slanted downward, as if falling into the earth.

William Gilbert of Colchester, England, published his great treatise on magnets, *De Magnete,*[6] in 1600, using references from Petrus Peregrinus's letter, as well as many of his own experimental observations. Gilbert's work became the authoritative text on magnets for the next hundred years, and encouraged many other "natural philosophers" throughout Europe to begin making experiments of their own with magnets. Between 1600 and 1609, Galileo performed a number of experiments with magnetism, referring in both conversation and correspondence with his friends to Gilbert's work, *De Magnete*. Gilbert's book introduced to the European scientific community the idea of lodestones as experimental objects. Gilbert had realized that Earth itself was one huge magnet, with its poles located (he assumed) at, or quite near, the geographical north and south poles.

Gilbert also assumed that iron lying exposed to Earth's magnetic field for many years would become magnetized by it. Indeed, it does, but then so does almost anything else that has magnetic properties. It is this characteristic of very many objects and materials that allows us to measure the changes in Earth's magnetic field that have occurred over the long eras of geological time. As scientific instrumentation used to measure magnetic fields became increasingly more sensitive, it became possible for scientists to measure increasingly weaker magnetic fields. This had the surprising result of revealing that almost everything on Earth has its own minute magnetic field surrounding it.

Gilbert had described another method of making magnets—heating an iron rod to a certain temperature, and then hammering it as it cooled. We now know that if iron is heated beyond a certain point, its Curie point (named after the French scientist, Pierre Curie, 1859–1906), it loses all magnetism. On being worked and cooled, the iron will retain the magnetic field existing around it. Naturally, this kind of a magnet is not nearly as strong as that which is formed in a lodestone by the electrical charge imposed on it by a lightning strike.

In 1635, Henry Gellibrand showed that the declination error between compass north and true north changed over time. This discovery meant that navigators had to constantly be aware of the change in the error of declination, as well as its rate of change over the passage of time. This required that local observations of the compass bearing to true north be made from time to time, so that the changes in the compass declination over time could be measured, and the rate of change calculated.

In 1692, Edmond Halley (of Halley's comet fame) described the process of generation of Earth's magnetic field by postulating that several layers of spheres existed inside the earth, each with their own field, and each rotating to generate Earth's magnetic field. Despite many objections to his description being raised over the course of time, scientists today have returned to a slightly more elegant explanation of Halley's original description of Earth's magnetic field.

Charles Coulomb of France, in 1777, discovered the "inverse square law," which shows that the force of a magnet is a bit like gravity, growing weaker in proportion to the distance from the pole of the magnet. This decline in force is represented by the formula $1/r^2$, where r is the distance from the pole of the magnet. When the distance between two attracting magnets is increased, the attracting force is reduced by the square of that distance. Coulomb also introduced the prototype of the magnetic detector, a magnetic needle suspended in balance on a string, which served that purpose for about the next 170 years.

The discovery of the magnetic field around an electrical wire was made by Hans Christian Oersted (1771–1851) of the University of Copenhagen in Denmark. This discovery, made in 1820, began slowly raising the awareness of magnetism from simply being a natural curiosity to being a force with practical applications. Oersted's initial discovery of the magnetic field around a wire carrying an electrical current was amplified by André Marie Ampère (1775–1836) of France, who passed current through loops of wire, forming electromagnets. He showed that the polarity of electrically-induced magnetism followed the same rules as the polarity of the natural lodestone magnets. We now know that whenever a current flows in a wire, there is a magnetic field formed around that wire. From this follows the concept that the motion of any charged particle will produce a magnetic field, a concept important in the science of electronics and nuclear physics.

Michael Faraday (1791–1867) of England discovered paramagnetism and diamagnetism by constructing a "great electromagnet." He also constructed the first electrical dynamo for generating electricity, and the first electrical motor. Faraday showed that there was a connection between magnetism and light, but it took the mathematical brilliance of James Clerk Maxwell to explain this most interesting relationship.

We can easily understand from this that Earth's magnetic field is in a constant state of change. Yet, there is another, more transient, influence on Earth's magnetic field. This is the presence of magnetic storms, which were discovered by Baron Alexander von Humboldt (1769–1859) of Berlin, Germany. In 1806 and 1807, he observed the exact direction that a compass needle was pointing every half hour between sunset and sunrise. On December 21, 1806, he found that strong magnetic disturbances caused the compass needle to move radically. That same night he also witnessed the aurora borealis, the northern lights, in the night sky. By morning, the compass needle was steady, and the aurora was gone. Humboldt had discovered the magnetic storm, a major disturbance of Earth's magnetic field.

Magnetic storms have a great influence on electromagnetic (radio and TV) communications, power distribution in the electrical grids that supply our homes and offices, and they may even seriously affect wired telephone cables. Magnetic storms are one of the primary causes of the aurora borealis.

Now we must note that these fluctuations in Earth's magnetic field are always fluctuations of intensity. During these fluctuations, the polarity of the magnetic field does not ever reverse. All that actually seems to happen to the compass is that the direction of the compass needle may move a bit. That these movements are usually quite small may be understood by the fact that von Humboldt used a microscope to note the very small movements of the needle of his compass. Even the most powerful magnetic storms barely move the compass needle, although they may cause electrical power outages, a breakdown in radio communications, and create considerable interference in radio, television, and satellite signals.

In 1828, von Humboldt, who had become quite interested in magnetism, met the great German mathematician, Carl Friedrich Gauss. Von Humboldt suggested to Gauss that he apply his considerable mathematical talents to unraveling the mysteries of magnetism. Gauss and his associate Weber then built a laboratory in which to study magnetism. There they discovered a way to measure the strength of a magnetic field. In the process, they developed the world's first magnetic telegraph. Gauss mathematically described Earth's magnetic field. He and Weber formed a "Magnetic Union" to record magnetic measurements around the globe. This effort, in which several nations eventually participated, resulted in the first global model of Earth's magnetic field.

Around 1830, a German pharmacist and amateur astronomer named Heinrich Schwabe discovered the 11-year sunspot cycle. It was soon determined that large magnetic storms, which slightly influenced the direction of the compass needle on both ships and land, were related to those years that had the most sunspots. In 1908, George Elery Hale determined that these sunspots were actually magnetic storms on the surface of the sun. The effect of these magnetic storms is carried to Earth by the "solar wind," which continually moves from the sun to Earth, carrying along photons of light, radiation of various kinds, and numerous free electrons.

Between 1862–1864 the interrelationship of electricity and magnetism was demonstrated by the brilliant Scottish mathematician, James Clerk Maxwell (1831–1879), through a set of deceptively simple-looking calculus equations. As his mathematical explanation showed that light was an electrical phenomenon as well, it opened the door to the application of electromagnetic theory, the later discovery of radio waves, and eventually, a great deal of what we know of today as modern physics. Maxwell was one of the greatest scientists, and made many contributions to our knowledge in a wide variety of fields.

In the 19th century, when dynamos made possible the generation of electricity in almost unlimited quantities, the practical use of electromagnets was soon discovered. Shortly thereafter, the effect of the magnetic field surrounding electrical wires was applied in the invention of the electrical motor. This single invention swiftly brought the ongoing industrial revolution into the electrical age.

In 1897, Sir Joseph John Thomson (1856–1940) discovered the electron. This fundamental discovery greatly increased our understanding of both electricity and magnetism. The discovery of the electron began to lay the theoretical foundation of modern physics, as well as opening the door to a greater understanding of the nature of chemical reactions.

Between the 12th and the mid-19th centuries, the study of magnets and magnetism was severely limited by the lack of good, permanent magnets to study. It was not until the early 20th century, and the discovery of ways to manufacture increasingly stronger permanent magnets, that the science of magnetics began to be a field of study in itself. Today we have a variety of different types and strengths of permanent magnets to use in our work. It is good to remember that before about the mid-20th century, this was just not so. Ancient tales of very strong magnets are just that, tales without any foundation in fact.

There always seems to be a tendency to credit ancient civilizations—including those which are entirely hypothetical, such as Atlantis and Mu—with amazing hidden or occult knowledge and almost miraculous powers, which the best scientific research to date cannot show that these people actually ever possessed or even imagined.

I have read an enthusiastic writer's description of how ancient Egyptian physician priests added powdered lodestones to their medicinal prescriptions. This is probably false, but even if it is true, we should also recall that these same ancient Egyptian physician-priests also added powdered spiders, dung beetles, dirt, the finely-ground dried organs of various animals, and all kinds of other distasteful things to their ineffective healing potions.

Until someone can show some contemporary documents that prove otherwise, I will now state categorically that the ancient Egyptians, and other contemporary ancient societies, had no real knowledge of magnets at all, either natural or manufactured. If they knew of lodestones at all, these were probably only a curiosity to them.

I do believe that it is quite safe to make this statement, as it is possible to draw whatever interpretation you may wish from the many pictures painted on the walls of the Egyptian tombs. This is particularly easy to do with those pictures you do not understand. One of these pictures has even been interpreted by a modern writer as being an ancient TV camera, others as showing spacemen walking in their bulky suits. Do not believe that the ancients had either powerful natural magnets, or electromagnets—they did not. If they worked with natural magnets, lodestones, at all, it was in great ignorance of what it was they were actually dealing with.

Franz Friedrich Anton Mesmer (1734–1815), the "magnetic healer" of the late 1700s, came onto the historical scene just as the magnetic effect of electrical current flow was being discovered. At the time, the medical profession (Mesmer was a physician, although he had first earned a Ph.D. in philosophy) was in a state of flux, as many forms of long-approved medical treatment were slowly being proven to be completely ineffective. As magnetism and its effects were all the rage of drawing-room conversation at that time, he called the techniques that he used to induce cures of psychosomatic conditions "magnetic." He even called the passes of his hands that he made over people "magnetic passes."

Mesmer's practice of "animal magnetism" actually had less to do with the application of magnetics than it did with the psychological influence of inducing belief, and the healing of psychosomatic complaints under rather dramatic conditions. In these conditions, compliance with a healing modality in the company of other believers is known to frequently take place. The same effects are found in charismatic healing church services held by many religious groups today, as well as in psychological group therapy sessions led by a dynamic person. Mesmer strongly believed that he magnetized objects of various kinds by exerting his own willpower and through the effect of his inherent personal ability. Later research has proven that he was largely correct in the belief that his personal charisma promoted cures.

Mesmer healed people through the dramatic group application of what he called "magnetic treatments." As a result, many magnetic devices used in both magic and healing today have an origin that is frequently credited to him, always incorrectly. Mesmer is also credited today with both the discovery and the initial application of hypnotism, although that phenomenon, first discovered among relatively few of Mesmer's patients, was uninvestigated, and even unrecognized, by him. Initially, hypnotic phenomena were both investigated and exploited by one of Mesmer's students and followers, the Marquis de Puysegur. Because of the great interest in Mesmer, and his relationship to magnetism, I have included a brief biography of his very interesting life in the appendix of this book.

There is a tendency for those interested in the occult sciences or the non-physical forces to credit the unknown forces of the invisible world to whatever the current fad of popular interest in the physical sciences happens to be. This may be easily seen in crediting the effects of Mesmer's dramatic displays to the animal variety of magnetism. This would be neither the first nor the last of the many attributions of non-physical effects to newly-discovered processes found in the physical sciences.

Once X rays were discovered, the enthusiastic but usually poorly educated occultist hopped onto the bandwagon of these mysterious rays, explaining all kinds of non-physical effects in terms of rays of various kinds. Next, the invention of radio communications caused many of the effects of the invisible world to be attributed to waves, because radio waves happened to be all the rage of drawing-room and dinner-table conversation at that time. Now we hear talk of vibrations, or "vibes." This followed the scientific discovery that every material thing has its own natural frequency of vibration. These are all attempts to explain something that is not well understood in terms that the speaker believes the listener may either understand, or at least have a passing familiarity with. Obviously, the attempted explanation is not correct in terms of what is true in the non-physical world.

Today magnetic fields, coming from both permanent and electromagnets, are used in a wide variety of ways in both business and industry. Magnets are used for energy conversion, for holding things, as in the magnetic chuck of the machine shop, levitation of things, as in the metallic "sheet separator" often found near the industrial punch press, and the transmission of torque (twisting force), as in the magnetic clutch. Magnets are even found in such applications as water purification and the control of erosion in pipes. It may be unromantic and disenchanting to point this out to the occult enthusiast, but the ancients knew of none of these many applications of magnets. Floppy disks as well as computer hard drives also work through the operation of the quite minute magnetic fields that are impressed upon them. Our credit cards, ATM cards, and even some of our identification cards that carry the band of magnetized material we know as the magnetic strip are also common applications of magnetic fields.

Not only did the ancients not know of these many applications, but as I have mentioned, the magnets that our scientifically-inclined ancestors of the 12th through the late 19th century had to work with were far weaker than the magnets that we have today. As we learn what can be accomplished with magnets in the occult arts, we must bear in mind that the magnets that we use today are far more powerful than anything of which Mesmer and his followers ever dreamed.

Magnetic healing has been all the rage recently, and while those who wish to gain some *bona fides* from their work often credit it to the ancients, it is actually a relatively new thing under the sun. There are a large number of firms that sell magnetic this and magnetic that, designed to relieve everything from constipation to backache. Promoters began widely advertising such magnetic devices in the late 19th century, when inexpensive manufactured magnets first became available. These magnetic healing devices have wavered in and out of public favor ever since.

It might be good to point out that there have been few or no published double-blind, peer-reviewed studies done on the subject of magnetic healing, or of magnetic therapeutic appliances.[7] This subject is still one of great debate. The American Medical Association, the American Food and Drug Administration, and the British Advertising Standards Agency all oppose the many claims being made for these magnetic products. The rather humorously named "Committee for the Scientific Investigation of the Claims of the Paranormal," has even gone so far to divert attention from its own internal difficulties as to have taken legal action against at least one manufacturer of a magnetic product.

How magnetic healing works is not only misunderstood, but there seems to be no real unanimous opinion concerning its application between the various people and groups who so enthusiastically espouse it. However, since it has been found that placebos heal patients in about 30 percent of the cases in which they are used, that fact alone may give us some insight into why many supposedly miraculous cures are reported from the application of magnets. I shall touch on magnetic healing later, in chapter 10, but only briefly. I see my physician when I find that I have any physical condition, and I suggest that you do the same.

One of the scientific facts that those who encourage the use of magnets in healing base their theories on is that Earth's magnetic field—at least the dominant north-south magnetic field (scientists have discovered several other considerably less important magnetic fields)—is getting weaker at the rate of about 5 percent each century, and the rate of decrease may have even increased since about 1970. Should this trend continue, some scientists expect that in another 2000 years or so, Earth's magnetic field would reverse.

However, should this ever occur, Earth's magnetic field would not disappear because the other magnetic fields discovered by scientists like Carl Friedrich Gauss of Germany (which he named the 4-pole, the 8-pole and so forth), are getting stronger as the dipole (2-pole) field weakens. As these changes in Earth's magnetism occur, it has been postulated that the total magnetic energy present on Earth would remain the same. What would change would be the dominant compass direction, something that has happened at least once over Earth's long geological history. Most recently, the poles reversed about 700,000 years ago. On the sun, the magnetic poles are thought to reverse their polarity about every eleven years, approximately in harmony with the sunspot cycle.

We should not be concerned about this potential reversal of Earth's magnetic poles, nor should we be overly concerned about the magnetic field weakening. Earth's magnetic field is a natural phenomenon over which humanity has no control at all. It is also something that is unlikely to be relieved in an individual by wearing magnetic jewelry, or by using magnetic appliances of any kind.

Magnetism directly affects not just compasses, but people, insects, birds, and many animals. There are magnetic bacteria, and it has been found that certain birds and even insects have a magnetic sense of direction. Professor Orley Taylor of the University of Kansas has shown that during their migration, monarch butterflies use magnetism (among other things, such as their biological clock and sunlight) to navigate. This explains the uncanny accuracy with which these frail creatures complete their annual migration journey of over 2,500 miles between the United States and Mexico.

Having explained some of the historical background of lodestones, magnets, and compasses, and having surveyed the history of the study of magnetism, we shall look at just what magnets are, and how it is that they seem to work.

CHAPTER 2

What You Need to Know about Magnets

In the last century, scientists have learned that every known thing on Earth is influenced to some degree by Earth's magnetic field, and that almost everything on Earth has a magnetic charge or a very slight magnetic field of its own. From the record of these magnetic fields, scientists with extremely delicate instruments have learned a great deal about Earth's geology, and its development over the long ages of geological time.

Scientists and magicians may work with magnets, using them to their advantage in many applications, but no one seems to have any real idea what a magnetic field actually is. As an approach to attempting to understand what a magnetic field is, we may say that magnetic properties seem to be found as the result of forces between electrical charges (such as are found in atoms and molecules) in motion. About all we do know now is that electricity and magnetism seem to be very closely related. Of course, this is a simplification; the physicist has a much more elegant explanation of the magnetic effect. Yet, even the physicist will usually come down to the simple definition of magnetism as electrical charges in motion.

So now we can define a magnet as something that has a magnetic field. That is not much of a definition, but by using it, we will find that we can apply magnetism in many ways. First, let us look at those things that are more obviously magnetic, or at least are the carriers of magnetic energy. Some substances can be induced to become magnetic. These substances are called ferromagnetic substances. They are named after *ferrum*, the Latin word for iron, the best known of these substances. We can divide these ferromagnetic substances into the "soft" ferromagnetics (or the temporary magnets), which lose their own magnetic field as soon as they are removed from the source of the magnetic field, and the "hard" ferromagnetics (or the permanent magnets), which can retain their magnetic field once they are magnetized. From the hard ferromagnetic materials we can make other permanent magnets, as permanent magnets are a source of magnetism. Naturally occurring lodestones are hard ferromagnetic substances that retain their magnetic field when they are out of contact with any other source of a magnetic field.

Magnets usually have two poles, a north-seeking pole, and a south-seeking pole. The north-seeking pole is usually referred to as the north pole, while the south-seeking pole is usually referred to as the south pole. We will identify the poles in this way, although other authorities may differ in their definition. You should be aware of this difference, and always be certain which poles of the magnet are actually being referred to in any material you may read concerning this matter.

Some manufactured magnets have three poles, in which case one of the poles is usually located between the other two poles. The possibility of a magnet with a

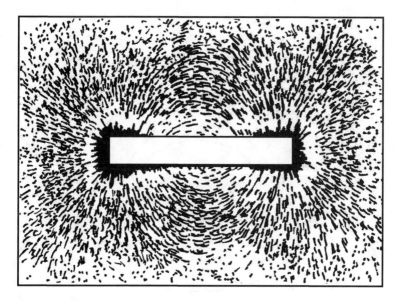

Fig. 1. Lines of force around a bar magnet as shown by iron filings

single pole (mono-pole magnets) is being actively investigated by scientists who deal with magnetic phenomena. We shall have nothing to do with three-pole magnets, and we probably will not be able to afford single-pole magnets should they ever be invented, so in this book we shall concern ourselves only with conventional two-pole magnets.

There are a few scientific laws that deal with magnets. We shall have to learn and remember them, as they are quite important for anyone working with magnets. The first law dealing with magnets that we must remember is the law of magnetic poles. This law tells us which poles of a magnet attract, and which repel.

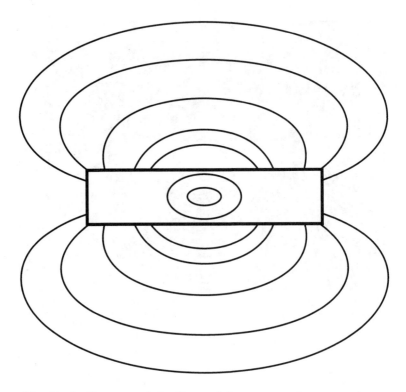

Fig. 2. A diagram of the lines of force around a magnet

The Law of Magnetic Poles

As first stated by Petrus Peregrinus in 1269, similar magnetic poles repel; opposite magnetic poles attract.

If two ends of a magnet are attracted to each other, it means that they have opposite poles; one of the poles is north, the other, south. We do not know which pole is which, but we do know that they are different poles. If the two ends of a magnet repel each other, we know that they are similar, or like, poles. Again, we do not know which pole they are, but we do know that the poles are similar. The law of magnetic poles is the most fundamental law of magnets.

A magnetic field is defined as being the region in space where the presence of a magnetic force can be detected. This is actually everywhere on Earth, not just in a magnet laboratory, as the Earth has its own magnetic field. However, the magnetic field around any magnet you may choose to work with is said to go out only as far as you can detect it. As your only instrument for detection is likely to be a compass, you will find that your magnet's field will not extend very far out at all. A compass detects the magnetic field of Earth itself, which is why it can give you a bad directional reading if you happen to have other magnets lying around when you try to take a compass reading. If you perform the following experiment with a bar magnet, a piece of glass or paper, and some iron filings, you will discover that the magnetic field of any magnet is always strongest at the poles of the magnet.

A Magnetic Field Experiment

For this experiment you will need a bar magnet, some iron filings, and a piece of glass or a sheet of typing paper.

Place the bar magnet on a table. Put the glass or sheet of paper over it, supported as best you can, so the paper does not droop at the ends or edges. Sprinkle some iron filings over the glass or paper. Notice the way that the filings arrange themselves. The lines of iron filings outline what is known as the magnetic lines of force. This is one way of indicating the presence of a magnetic field. Notice that the lines of force do not ever cross.

The iron filings you are using might cross, especially if they are iron slivers and not powder, but magnetic lines of force never cross; they always form complete loops. These lines of force originate in the magnet, and they always terminate in the same magnet from which they originate.

The stronger the magnetic field, the closer together the lines of force are. In fact, there are always magnetic lines of force between the lines shown by the iron filings or powder. It is just not as easy to detect all of these lines of force, as the iron filings are converted temporarily into little magnets of their own, and as they are parallel, and have the same magnetic polarity on their ends, these small temporary magnets repel each other.

It is also possible to symbolize the magnetic lines of force around a magnet by drawing lines indicating where iron filings would be found if they were applied. As you will discover, should you actually perform the experiment above, iron filings can be quite messy to work with.

Scientists have decided (without any real proof, but they had to agree on something in this matter) that the magnetic lines of force flow (or point) from the north pole to the south pole outside of the magnet, and from the south pole to the north pole inside of the magnet.

This kind of decision is known as a conventional definition. There are many of these conventional definitions to be found in both the field of physical science and the field of non-physical forces, which we may call the hidden, or the occult. Conventional definitions describe something that it may not be possible either to prove or to disprove.

As an example, I have not heard or read anywhere that magnetic fields actually flow, as an electrical current is said to flow. However, for convenience in understanding them, magnetic fields are sometimes assumed to flow.

One explanation of magnets is that within certain materials, such as the hard ferromagnetic materials, the individual atoms and molecules may align themselves in a certain way, and then maintain that alignment indefinitely. Thus inside every permanent magnet are assumed to be millions of small, almost molecule-sized, magnets that are oriented pole to pole, in the same way that the larger magnet is. What is known is that if you break a permanent magnet, you will have a number of permanent magnets. Each piece of the former magnet now becomes a magnet in itself.

Earth's magnetic poles do not coincide with Earth's rotational axis, or the geographic poles. In other words, the north magnetic pole is not to be found at the geographic North Pole. To complicate matters a bit more, Earth's magnetic field varies in intensity and, to a lesser extent, in direction, all over Earth. This variation is due to such things as the presence of metallic ores in the earth, the elevation of the site above sea level, and the relationship of the other bodies in the solar system (particularly the sun) to Earth at the time that the magnetic reading is being taken. However, all of these magnetic fluctuations are minor, and most of them are extremely small. For our purposes, we will completely ignore all of these slight magnetic fluctuations.

Understanding Magnetic Poles and Magnetic Declination

Magnetic poles are defined by the direction in which they point in Earth's magnetic field. There has always been a lot of confusion on this point, so I shall first state it, and then I shall illustrate it.

> The north-pointing pole of a magnet points north, to Earth's south magnetic pole, which is located in the Northern Hemisphere.
>
> The south-pointing pole of a magnet points south, to the Earth's north magnetic pole, which is located in the Southern Hemisphere.

When we refer to the north pole of a magnet, we mean the north-pointing pole, and when we refer to the south pole of a magnet, we are referring to the south-pointing pole. As I have mentioned, other books may take a different view of the poles. Be certain that you know which pole you are reading about when you read books about magnetism, especially those books dealing with magnetic healing.

Figure 3 on page 27 may clarify this somewhat confusing subject. If you think of Earth as being a hollow ball inside of which someone has put a bar magnet, you will get an idea about the way magnetic poles work inside our Earth. The hollow ball rotates around an axis, but the magnet inside the ball is not aligned exactly with the axis of the ball's rotation. Now assume that every once in a while the magnet slips a little bit inside of the hollow ball. The axis of rotation may change a little bit over time as well, but the magnet's axis and the hollow ball's rotational axis just never seem to coincide. Thinking of it in that way, you can understand that if you are on the ball—our Earth—and you use a compass that is pointing to the north magnetic pole, it will not necessarily be pointing to the geographic North Pole.

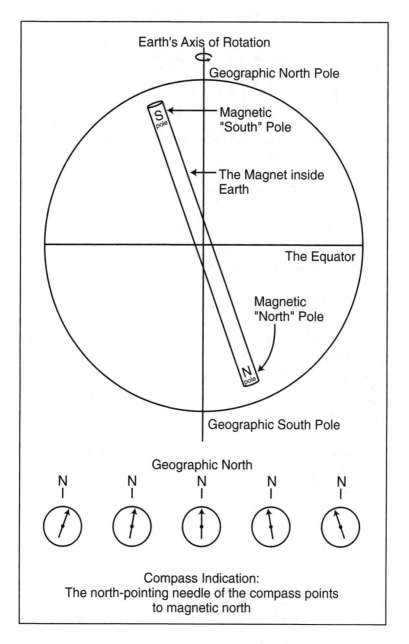

Fig. 3. The magnetic and geographic poles

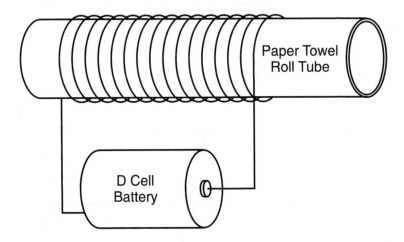

Fig. 4. A tube electromagnet

The axis of Earth's rotation is the north and south geographic poles. The angle measured between the geographic and the magnetic poles, which is slightly different for all of the various points on this earth, is known as the magnetic declination (or sometimes as the compass error).

Once you understand this concept, you may wish to learn the magnetic declination for your own location on Earth. The easiest way to learn this is to go to your public library and look at a topographic map of your location. Almost all topographic maps show a "declination correction index" somewhere in their margin. The large-scale maps published by the United States Coast and Geodetic Survey have this information in the lower left-hand portion of their margin. There are also special maps that show the approximate magnetic declination over a wide area. These are called isogonic maps, and are available for the United States in the many Government

Document Depository Libraries, which are usually found in large cities.

In the United States, magnetic declination (in 1999) varies from zero in parts of Wisconsin to approximately +14 degrees in New York City and to approximately -14 degrees in San Diego, California. Over the entire country, the declination varied from +21 degrees to -22 degrees. In addition to this variation, there is usually stated on these maps a rate of change, which indicates approximately how much the magnetic declination of the area covered by the map increases or decreases each year.

Permanent Magnetic and Electromagnetic Fields

A permanent magnet has an unchanging magnetic field. The north pole of a permanent magnet is always the north pole; the south pole is always the south pole. An electromagnet is created by the application of electricity to a coil of wire. If we change the polarity of the voltage being applied to an electromagnet, we can change the poles of the magnetic field. If we apply an alternating current to a coil of wire, we will find that the poles of the magnet will reverse, as the alternating current goes from positive to negative.

An Electromagnetic Experiment

Take a cardboard tube, such as is found at the center of a roll of paper towels. Wind several turns of fine copper wire, such as is used to wire a doorbell, around the outside of this cardboard tube. You now have the beginnings of an electromagnet. If you place a compass at the end of the tube, and connect a dry cell flashlight battery to the ends of the wire as shown in figure 4. (DO NOT connect this coil to an electrical outlet!), you will find that either the north or south pole of your compass will point to the end of the coil of wire. Now reverse the polarity by switching the wires connected to your battery. You will see the compass needle pointing to the coil reverse itself.

This is essentially the same experiment that Ampère performed, demonstrating that the magnetism created by electricity in a coil of wire was the same as that which was found in a lodestone, or a natural magnet.

The Magnetic Field

Whether we are dealing with the magnetic field of a permanent magnet, or that of an electromagnet, we must bear in mind that the magnetic field of any magnet originates and terminates in the magnet that is its source. If we have two magnets, we may not get the magnetic field of one to flow through the other. If we look at magnetic fields as energy sources, we can understand that the energy originates there, and must return to the source of its origin. Thus, each permanent magnet must be considered to have its own magnetic field, and to be a self-contained source of magnetic energy. Even when two magnets are firmly held together by their mutual attraction, their magnetic fields meet, but they do not interchange. The magnetic fields remain separate and distinct in all cases.

Aside from those materials that are strongly attracted to magnetic fields (the ferromagnetics), many materials are only weakly attracted to magnetic fields. These materials are known as paramagnetic materials. When magnetic attraction is present, but it is so weak as to deny their being ferromagnetic, the materials are known as paramagnetic. Some of the rare earth elements have this characteristic, as do a few others. These elements are said to have a magnetic dipole, or a very slight magnetic characteristic.

Having positive and relatively neutral elements in the magnetic range of things, we would also expect to find negative elements as well. In many materials, the magnetic effects of the electrons exactly cancel out, so the electrons of the atom or molecule are not magnetic at all. This is true for copper, as one example. These are not paramagnetic materials. These elements are known as diamagnetic, which means that they are very weakly repelled by a magnetic field. Carbon, copper, lead, silver, mercury, gold, antimony, and bismuth are all diamagnetic substances. Bismuth is generally regarded as being the most strongly diamagnetic substance. Many complex organic substances, including human blood, are also diamagnetic. Diamagnetic substances behave as if they were "anti-magnets"; they tend to align themselves against the magnetic lines of force. Like magnetism itself, diamagnetism is also found in all substances, but usually with a very feeble effect. Strongly diamagnetic materials are repelled from the poles of a strong magnet, while ferromagnetic and paramagnetic materials would be respectively strongly and weakly attracted to the poles of the same magnet.

The positive ferromagnetics, iron, cobalt, and nickel, as well as two far rarer materials, gadolinium and terbium, have the unusual property that the adjacent atoms in the material can form a rigid coupling, bringing the atoms into a kind of parallel alignment. This is what gives these materials their magnetic effect. However, if the temperature of these materials is raised above a certain point, known as the Curie temperature for the material, the alignment of the atoms suddenly disappears, and the material just as suddenly becomes paramagnetic. The Curie temperature for iron is about 800 degrees Fahrenheit. This sudden change in magnetism indicates that the property of ferromagnetism correlates to the interchange of energy between the individual atoms, something that occurs within the solid material itself.

Further proof of the way that magnets are formed is shown by the fact that there are magnetic alloys, some of which contain little or no iron. An example is an alloy consisting of 65% copper, 25% manganese, and 10 % aluminum. These alloys prove that magnetism is not simply the inherent property of some elements, but is actually caused by the internal electronic arrangement of the atoms and molecules in the substance.

Permalloy, made of 55% iron and 45% nickel, is an example of a magnetic alloy containing iron. Supermalloy, 15.7% iron, 79% nickel, 5% molybdenum, and 0.3% manganese, is another. Mu Metal, which is often used as a magnetic shield, contains 77% nickel, 16% iron, 5% copper, and 2% chromium, is a third. Alnico, which makes a considerably stronger magnet than pure iron, is composed of iron, aluminum, cobalt, and nickel.

Some ferromagnetic substances are not metallic— ferrites, a mixture of iron and other metallic oxides are an example of this. Lodestones contain magnetite, an oxide of iron, which is a nonmetallic ferromagnet.

Today, powerful ceramic magnets made from rare earth elements are available, although they are quite fragile and usually rather expensive.

Magnetizing Iron

Any hard ferromagnetic material may be magnetized by repeatedly stroking it in the same direction with the same pole of a permanent magnet. The magnetism that is induced in this way in an object like a sewing needle or a pin is said to be "remnant magnetism." Soft ferromagnetic materials do not retain their magnetism when removed from the influence of the magnet. These materials are said to have low remnant magnetism.

Another way to magnetize something is to place it within a coil of wire and then apply a direct current, or a dry cell battery, to the coil. The magnetic force applied to the item in the coil is directly proportional to the product of the number of turns of wire in the coil, and the current flowing thorough the coil, as expressed in the following formula:

Magnetic Force = Number of Turns x Current (in amps)

Since the number of turns in any wire coil is always proportional to the resistance of the coil (for any given size of wire, the more turns, the greater the resistance) we may also say that the magnetizing force of the coil is equal to I x R, or the current times the resistance. This, incidentally, gives us the direct current voltage that must be impressed on the coil to gain the current desired.

This is a calculation of Ohm's Law, a fundamental law in electrical theory. Ohm's Law relates the three principal

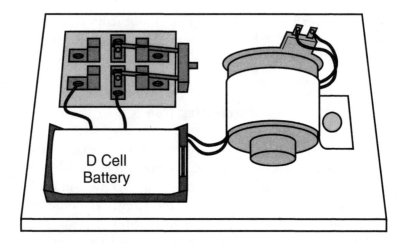

Fig. 5. A magnetizing device

constituents—voltage, current, and resistance—of direct current electrical circuits, as found in those operated by a battery. According to Ohm's Law:

Voltage = Current x Resistance

As most electromagnet coils are wound with fine wire, the current that they will carry is quite limited. It is best to limit the current to an ampere, or possibly even less. It is also important to avoid heating the coil, as that may cause the fine wire of the coil to burn out, rendering the coil useless. You can make a device to magnetize small steel objects, such as sewing needles, out of the coil of a magnetic solenoid valve and a dry cell. You might find such a device useful in making your own magnetic needles for further experimentation. See figure 5.

Chapter 3

Magnets in Daily Life

Magnetic strips on bank cards, credit cards, and similar cards, as well as the floppy disks and hard drives of computers, are magnetized by very small currents passing through very fine coils of wire. These magnetized strips are "read" by the electrical signals received when these same coils of wire pass over the magnetized strip or disk. The electricity in the coil induces magnetism in the magnetic iron oxide material of the strip or disk to magnetize it. Then a similar coil senses the magnetic signal sent by the electrical current induced in the coil moving over the magnetic field, as the cards are swiped, passed through the card reader, or read by the drive in the computer. The material in these computer disks and magnetic cards is quite similar to the kind of iron oxide that is found in a natural lodestone. We could even say that these magnetic marvels are our modern-day magnetic charms.

There are a number of rather interesting magnetic devices that you can make for reasonably useful purposes around the home. Although these projects are not at all particularly exotic, they do have the benefit of introducing someone interested in working with magnets to a few simple projects. I have first included a project that is obviously more suitable for the home-owner than the apartment dweller. From there we shall go on to projects that are more in the realm of the magician, as well as those who work with plants and take delight in growing things.

A Magnetic Combustion Improvement & Water Scale Elimination Device

From time to time advertisements have appeared in various magazines touting a magnetic fuel-saving device, which is said to improve your automobile's gas mileage. Similar advertisements have also appeared concerning magnetic devices said to de-scale your water pipes, and prevent further scaling. While many of these devices have been sold, their real efficiency may be judged by the fact that most of the manufacturers of these magnetic devices have either gone on to sell something else or have gone bank-rupt. There is obviously not a big money market waiting for these magnetic devices.

However, there was (about 15 years ago) at least one manufacturer of a water-cooled air compressor that provided a magnetic "de-scaler" for its water-cooled condensers. This manufacturer claimed that the device extended the life of the condensers tenfold. In operation, the device was supposed to align the paramagnetic molecules of the solids in the water so that they would not form scale in the small-diameter pipes of the condenser. Like all manufacturers of these devices, this manufacturer had a variety of letters from satisfied customers proving its value. As his magnetic device did not interfere with the operation of his water-cooled condenser, it could certainly do it no harm.

Should you wish to add a magnetic combustion improvement device, or a magnetic de-scaler, to either your fuel or water supply, here are a few salient points to observe in doing so. These are taken both from the manufacturer's literature concerning these devices, as well as the experience of one of my former students who has built and installed several of them in his automobiles and other appliances.[8]

Magnetic Combustion Improvement Device and De-scaler Instructions

Warning: Should this process be the least bit unfamiliar to you, please do not attempt to modify your automobile or your home heating system yourself. It could be quite dangerous, and possibly result in a fire, or even an explosion. This is actually work for a professional skilled tradesperson. I have been assured that a skilled tradesperson will understand the following instructions.

- The magnets must be located as close as possible to the place where the fuel is either atomized or burned. This requires that, for gasoline engines, the magnets should be located on the fuel line, as close as possible to the carburetor. For oil burners, they should be located immediately at the input to the oil burner. For gas stoves or heating appliances, the magnets should be located as close as possible to the gas connection to the appliance.

- Ideally, the magnets should be attached to plastic, brass, or copper pipe. Placing magnets on a steel pipe will cause them to attempt to magnetize the entire pipe. This defeats the purpose of having an intense magnetic field through which the water or fluid may flow. The intense magnetic field is what would be required to induce magnetism in the paramagnetic solids found in the fuel or water.

- If it is necessary to install magnets on a steel pipe, a pair of dielectric unions (available at plumbing supply stores or large home improvement stores), which block the transmission of small electrical currents and the magnetic field, may be placed on either side of the magnets. To maintain the required electrical ground of the piping system, grounding clamps and a large-gauge jumper wire should be used.

- The magnets you use should be strong bar magnets that have their poles on their ends. This allows the magnetic field, which goes all around the magnet, to penetrate into the pipe.

- The number of magnets used should be proportional to the trade size of the pipe. Obviously, the larger the pipe's diameter, the more magnets it will require. I think that at least two bar magnets should be used on all but the very smallest of pipes.

- Within reason, the stronger the permanent magnets you use, the better the device will operate.

- Now for the big secret, given to me by a plumber from Australia, who says that only in this way will the device actually work as it is supposed to: The flow of the fluid that is being treated through the magnetic field *must* be from the north-pointing pole of the magnets to the south-pointing pole. See figure 6.

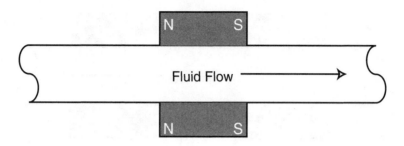

Fig. 6. A magnetic device for water or fuel

I must add that in areas where the water has a very high iron content, this device will be completely ineffective. In this case, the water must first be passed through an iron removal filter. Placing an iron removal filter on your water supply is a good idea anyway, as excessive iron in your cooking and drinking water can be detrimental to your health.

If you are uncertain of the strength of your magnets, or you want to be sure that you get the full magnetic effect from the treatment, place two sets of magnets in a series on the fluid feed line, spacing them about two inches—or at least the length of one of the magnets— apart. See figure 7.

Using Magnetically-Charged Water

I had a magnetic charging pad sitting on my kitchen counter one bright summer day. Being thirsty, I went to the sink for a glass of water. Just after I drew the water, the doorbell rang, requiring me to walk down two flights

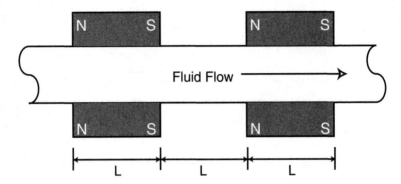

Fig. 7. Using multiple magnets on a pipe or tube when magnetizing water or fuel

of stairs and then come upstairs again. I found that I had absent-mindedly left the glass of water sitting on the charging pad. As I was now even thirstier than I had been previously, I drank the water, and I was surprised by its pleasant taste.

Despite the fact that New York City tap water supposedly once won first prize in a taste test over several varieties of bottled water, I had never felt that it was that exceptional a product. However, the "magnetic water," if I may call it that, had a definitely better taste than the usual tap water. After quenching my thirst, I experimented with two glasses of water. One I set on my kitchen counter, the other on the magnetic charging pad. I left both of them there for thirty minutes. Then I tasted them both. To my taste, the "magnetized" water seemed more clear and fresh tasting. It might be a useful experiment to try if you wish. I must admit that I do not keep magnetized water as my staple beverage. From time to time, I do have a glass, and I have been known to charge up a pitcher of water for occasional company.

Making a Water-Charging Magnet

Hearing of my adventure with the magnetized water, one of my students made what he called a water-charging magnet, which was basically a magnet set into a piece of wood, which was suitably finished for the table. If you want to have magnetized water, or any other magnetized beverage, you may want to make one for yourself. Figure 8 illustrates a plan of the one that sits on my table. It will have to be modified for the size of magnet you choose to use.

According to my student, you cut the wood to size first, and then use a chisel or router to make the hole for the magnets. Then you sand the block and glue the magnets in place. The final step is finishing the wooden block with three coats of polyurethane varnish, sanding lightly with fine steel wool between each coat. Cut a thin piece of felt to size and glue it to the bottom of the finished piece. The poles of the magnets he used are on the long side of each magnet, and it was made with the north-pointing poles facing the top of the piece. If nothing else, it is an afternoon's project for a handyperson, and it makes an interesting conversation piece. However, because polyurethane varnish can be easily scorched, the magnetic block should not be used as a hot plate.

Magnetic House Plants?

Watering houseplants with magnetically-charged water seems to have some benefit for them. I have also found some slight benefit from sprouting mung bean seeds in magnetically-charged water. One year a friend convinced

Top view

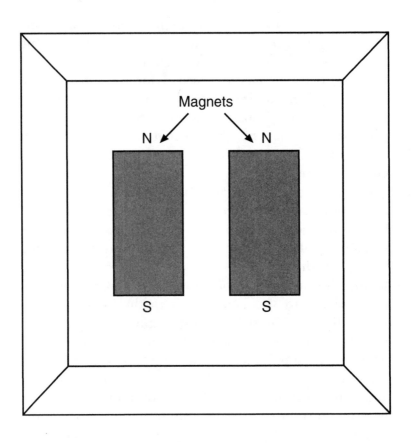

Cross-section view

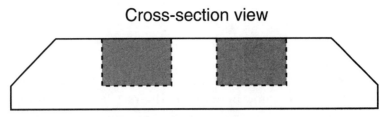

Fig. 8. A magnetic charging pad

me to grow some tomato plants. I watered them every day with magnetized water, just to see what kind of a harvest I could get. Although the window in my living room faces south, it is fairly well blocked by the building next door. Nonetheless, I managed to raise such a crop of tomatoes from only three tomato plants that I was soon encouraging all of my friends and students to take some of the harvest home with them. Whether this was due to the magnetic water or not, I have no idea, as I ran no control on this experiment.

I tried this with bean plants the following year, but the vines grew all over my living room window, obscuring the window itself. As a result, I ended the experiment before I was able to harvest any beans. But I did get to enjoy the flowers. I really believe that this is a better project for a suburban gardener than for someone attempting to grow a few plants in a plastic bucket, in a small apartment. If you decide to try this project, I would also suggest that you grow some control plants watered with regular tap water along with the ones watered with magnetized water. Only by using this type of control can you tell if there is actually a difference in the plants grown with magnetized water.

While we may think of the magnetic catches on our kitchen cabinets or the magnets we use to hold notes on our refrigerator as being useful and convenient additions to our life, we may also look at the magnetic devices mentioned in this chapter as having some value for us. Although these devices are not nearly as exotic or interesting as the magnetic devices mentioned in the following chapter, they still can add some interest to our home, even if only as conversation pieces. Naturally, as with all magnetic devices, you must be careful to keep these domestic devices away from that most interesting modern appliance, the personal computer. Setting one of your floppy disks on your magnetic charging pad will ruin all of the data on it in the blink of an eye. While the same is true of the magnetic devices in the next chapter, I have found that computers and magic seem to stay away from each other naturally. Of course, introducing computer media to any magnet is courting a data disaster.

CHAPTER 4

Magical Folklore of Magnets

Some people believe that lodestones are living rocks. From an animist standpoint, even a rock has a spirit of life inside it. The natural magnetic ability of lodestones is what gives people the belief that lodestones themselves are alive in some way. Since lodestones were first discovered in ancient times, they have been objects of curiosity, interest, and fascination. It is no wonder that those who found them originally used them for magical purposes.

Attracting Things Desired

As lodestones attract small bits of iron, they are frequently used in folk magic to attract the various things that the person working with them might desire. Lodestone magical charms have been found in the area of ancient Sumer (southern modern-day Iraq). The charm I have heard about was inscribed with the name of the god Marduk, one of whose appellations, or praise names, was "he who works at a distance." This is certainly a fit attribute for lodestones.

A lodestone's attracting quality is also perceived to be able to attract people to the one wearing it. Because of this, lodestone charms have occasionally been worn by prostitutes to attract customers. Some prostitutes have reported having good success with a lodestone charm, which they carry in a red charm bag either tucked in their bra or attached to the seam of their underwear. This is certainly a less dangerous spell for them to use than those spells using the toxic bluestone (copper sulfate).

The lodestone's attractive power is thought to be useful in attracting a lover. When a man places a lodestone on or under his bed, it is supposed to draw a woman to the bed. There is no equivalent ancient spell for a woman, as women were supposed to want to call a husband to themselves, rather than just a casual lover. That is why most lodestone charms for women deal with attracting a man for marriage rather than casual sex.

Men who place a lodestone in oil, and then anoint their genitals with the oil, are supposedly able to increase their sexual virility. This is probably a popular application, as magnetic, or lodestone oil, is found for sale in most occult and spiritual supply stores. In Mexico, lodestones are frequently worn by men in their belt buckles, supposedly to increase sexual performance.

Charms made of lodestones are supposed to increase luck at gambling. The idea is that they attract winnings to the one using them. Lodestones placed under the seat of a chair, or placed in a throne, were said to draw both wealth and love to the person sitting on them.

The lodestone charm, in which a lodestone is made for a particular purpose, and then "fed" with iron filings on a regular schedule, is so common in folk magical practices that chapter 5 is dedicated entirely to a few of the almost infinite varieties of this well-known charm. The one thing that they all have in common is that they are used to attract something that the person making the charm, or the one using it, desires to have as their own.

Modern Magical Applications

More powerful modern magnets may replace all of these lodestone charms. While they are not as magical or natural looking, they may be used for the same purpose. As but one example, placing a magnet in your bed is more powerfully accomplished with a modern, powerful ceramic or rare earth magnet than with a lodestone. If the magnet is placed on an iron bed frame, or on iron bedsprings, it will essentially radiate a magnetic field around your bed—a weak magnetic field to be sure, but probably one that is as strong as or even a bit stronger than Earth's magnetic field at that location. If you use one of the modern ceramic magnets, which are very powerful, you may even be able to detect the change you have made in your bedroom's magnetic field with your compass.

Measuring Changes in the Magnetic Field

Before altering the magnetic field in your bedroom, determine, with a good compass, where magnetic north is, and then take several readings at different points in the room. Usually readings taken at the four corners and in the center of the room will suffice.

Now change the magnetic field, by attaching a powerful magnet to the iron bed frame.

Take your compass readings again, and see if there has been any change in the deflection of the compass needle. This is usually a rather small change; a change of a degree is exceptional. A change of even less than a half-degree is sufficient and the change may be considerably smaller than that. If you detect any change at all with your compass, it is to be attributed to the change you have made in your local magnetic field.

Several commercial organizations sell magnetic pads for different sizes of beds. These pads are supposed to promote restful sleep and contribute to the healing of a variety of physical problems. I tend to doubt their claims, although all of these organizations have the usual collection of interesting reviews and enthusiastic letters from users, always praising their product. Attaching a magnet to the iron bed frame for magical purposes makes at least as much sense to me as sleeping on a pad of magnets for reasons of health. It probably results in a less lumpy sleeping surface, as well. I wonder if placing a magnetic pad on the bed for better sleep increases the number of people drawn to that bed! Somehow, I doubt it, as it is placed there with a different intent, and intention and symbolism are everything in practicing magic.

General Concepts for Practicing Magnet Magic

Magnetic charms, made with modern metallic and composite ceramic magnets have a similar effect to those charms made with natural lodestones. Over time, I have found that these modern magnets are considerably easier to work with.

A friend of mine was unemployed and he told me he needed money. I obtained a picture of him wearing a business suit, and placed the north pole of a horseshoe magnet over a silver dime that was located on the picture approximately in the area of his suit coat pocket. I just let the south pole of the magnet sit off to the side of his picture. I actually forgot about doing this for a week or so, and on noticing this arrangement again, I called him. He had just been engaged for a project that would last for at least two years and would pay him a decent income. His starting date was three days away, so I decided that I would leave the magnet in place for another week. His employment condition did not change any further, so I then disassembled the spell.

So far as which pole of a magnet to use, I have found that the north-pointing pole seems to be the one that draws the best when you wish to attract things either to yourself or to someone else. Of course, you often have no real choice in this matter if you are using a horseshoe magnet, where it is often difficult to use one pole without also using the other. I once purchased a dozen or so magnets about an inch wide by almost a half inch thick, and about two inches long. The magnets' poles were located on the ends. I used these magnets quite successfully by applying them to photographs placed on the top of a small steel shelving unit, which otherwise held only some boxes full of books.

In most cases, I would write out what the person wished to attract to themselves and place this written request over their photograph. Then I would place the north pole of the magnet on the written request, holding the request to the person's photograph. My success rate with spells of this sort was somewhat greater than 50 percent, which I considered adequate, taking into account the nature of some of the requests made by those for whom I was doing the work. By limiting their requests to what they might logically expect to obtain from the universe, my success rate with these simple spells grew closer to 75 percent.

Winning the Lottery—Working with the Sphere of Availability

As one quite common example, many people wish to win the lottery, but they try only for the very large prizes. These large prizes are usually outside of their sphere of availability. A person's sphere of availability determines what he or she may obtain from the universe at that time. People should attempt to gain the smaller lottery prizes first. Winning fifty dollars is far more likely than winning several million dollars at any game of chance, regardless of what game it might be.

At one time, when the state lottery was initiated in New York, I was frequently asked to assist people in winning it. Once I began telling them that they should wager on the three-digit number rather than on the million-dollar prize, most of their interest in getting my help quickly dropped off. Frankly, I did not miss those requests. The odds of winning any substantial amount in any of the state lotteries is somewhat less likely than your chance of being struck by lightning as you walk down the street. When you wager on a three-digit number, you have a much better chance of at least winning your wager back.

Incidentally, my favorite gambling charm is the nutmeg spell, which I have written about on page 103 in my book, *Century of Spells*. It does not contain a magnet or any part of a lodestone at all. I will add that the extent of my winnings in gambling has not ever been great, but then I have only rarely gambled at anything. If you wish to win, you have to play the lottery frequently.

Gaining a Lover

So far as attracting a lover is concerned, I generally recommend that people pray for the lover that they need. To enhance this prayer, I have occasionally suggested that they place the north pole of a small disk magnet over their third eye—in the center of their forehead—as they make their prayer. This seems to make the prayer more real to them, or to put it another way, it seems to increase their chances of success. At least two young ladies are now reasonably happily married as the result of making such prayers. They were both nice enough to let me know of the success with the prayers that they made.

Not everyone tells me what the success of my work has been. When I do not hear of favorable results, I tend to assume that the work was probably unsuccessful. Occasionally, I eventually discover that this was not the case at all; the person just did not bother to tell me of the favorable results that they had obtained. Should you not be aware of it, magicians always like to hear of the results of their work, successful or not.

Magnetic Charm Bags

Using lodestones or magnets in charm bags (also known as mojo bags or mojos) seems to increase the power of the charm. Of course, you want to be certain that everything you put into the charm bag is something that you wish to have increased or attract to yourself. Some simple examples of this would be to use a magnet with a silver dime to attract money, or placing a magnet with a cinnamon stick and other herbs to attract love, or putting a magnet with cinquefoil herb for improving your speaking or writing abilities.

I once made a charm of a magnet attached to a piece of amber. It was successfully used in attracting a lover for a rather plain looking woman in her mid-thirties. I also successfully used a small magnet along with a small quartz crystal in a charm bag to help someone increase their mental clarity.

I have mentioned only a few of the ways in which a magnet or a lodestone can be used to add attracting power to a charm. With some research into the magical properties of herbs, stones, and crystals, and the use of your imagination, the number of magnetic charms you can make is unlimited. I suggest Ms. Catherine Yronwode's book, *Hoodoo Herb and Root Magic* for guidance in selecting herbs for charm bags, magnetic or otherwise.

When making up charms of this kind I use some very small circular magnets, which you can get in a store that sells supplies for schoolteachers, or in a large hardware store. When using silver dimes and amber beads or crystals that have holes in them, I connect the bead or the dime to the circular magnet with a small piece of copper wire. Then I pray over the finished piece, and place the assembly into a red flannel charm bag. In my mind at least, this connects the magnet with what the person wearing it desires to draw to him or her.

Using magnets with seals and sigils in charm bags is another interesting process that I have found to be quite effective. In this case, I carefully draw the seal or sigil I am going to use on a piece of heavy paper, and then attach it to the north pole of a circular magnet with model airplane glue. I have found that it is important to learn all of the attributes of the spirit or entity whose seal or sigil you are going to use before you make the charm. Books such as *The Key of Solomon the King, The Book of the Sacred Magic of Abramelin the Mage,* and other grimoires will provide you plenty of information and examples to chose from.

Another interesting effect is that the magnets glued to seals and sigils in these charms may lose their power after a while. This is something I have been assured is quite normal, as the entity whose seal or sigil is used draws energy from the magnet. A prayer over the completed sigil or seal and magnet assembly directs the work of the entity onto the path desired.

Magnet Oil

Magnet oil is an interesting product. It usually takes long exposure to the magnet to affect any major change in the non-physical qualities of oil. Water seems to respond to the magnetizing effort much faster. One of my longtime students is a professional chemist, and he once ran a series of tests with olive oil. He easily convinced me that it takes at least a week to gain any real change in the nature of olive oil when it was exposed to the magnet. As with many other things, he also found that oil that is left cooling in the refrigerator while it was being magnetized took on a greater magnetic charge, and was more potent than oil that had been left outside and exposed to summer temperatures.

Of course, oil exposed to the summer's heat in a non-air-conditioned apartment often goes rancid. Magnetized or not, it is not a good idea to use rancid oils in magical work. This is why I keep a large number of things in my refrigerator that are not at all suitable to use as food!

To magnetize oil, I either used to just expose it to the magnet, by placing a small bottle on a magnetizing pad (see page 42), or by pouring some of it into a watch glass placed on the magnetizing pad. I now do this in the refrigerator, with the magnetizing pipe device described below. The results seem to have improved to some extent. Magnetized oil, to my non-physical senses, seems more "orderly" than its un-magnetized equivalent. I have been thinking about how best to describe this effect, and that is about the best description I can find. Magnetized water looks to me to be a bit lighter, astrally, than tap water, but that is, like all perceptions of the non-physical world, a subjective perception.

Making a Magnetizing Pipe

You can use this device for charging powders, oils, or water. You will need a piece of wood about 4" square, and 3/4" thick, a fitting known as a floor flange threaded for 3/4" pipe, and a 5 1/2" long piece of 3/4" pipe, in addition to at least two magnets and electricians' tape. The floor flange is mounted on the wooden block with appropriate screws, and the pipe is screwed into the floor flange.

Place two magnets on the pipe with the north-seeking end of the magnets up. Use electrical tape or "wire ties" to hold the magnets in place. This is not shown in figure 9.

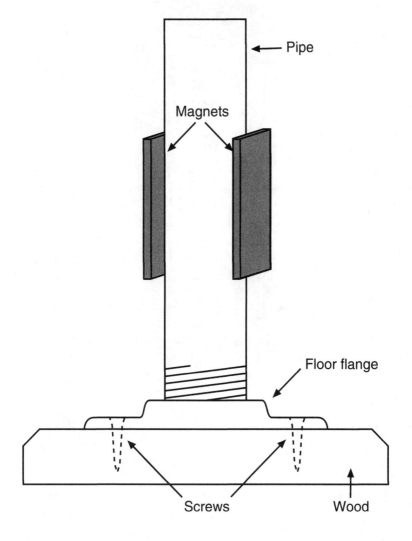

Fig. 9. *A magnetizing pipe*

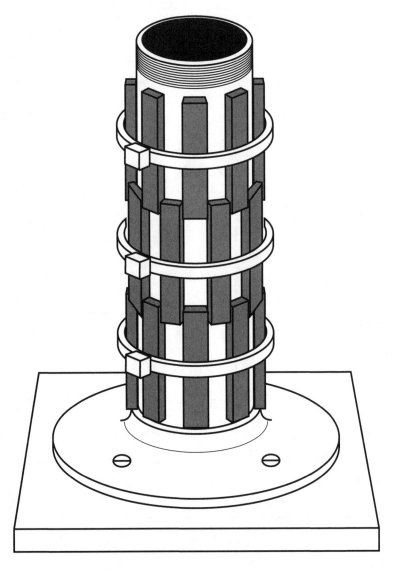

Fig. 10. Multiple magnets strapped to a pipe

The material to be charged is placed inside a glass tube, which is then put inside the piece of pipe. It's a good idea to cork the tube to keep out moisture from the refrigerator. The whole assembly is then placed inside the refrigerator for a week or more.

The magnetization effect is obtained by two or three of the magnets I previously described, which are taped to the outside of the piece of pipe with black electrical tape. I attempted to tape four magnets to the pipe, but as they are all in the same direction, north poles on top, their strong mutual repulsion forced me to settle for taping three of them to the pipe. With some strong metal clamps, you might be able to strap more magnets to the pipe (see figure 10). I have found this to be an interesting and quite worthwhile device. Should you be interested in magnetizing powders, waters, or oils, I suggest that you make one of these simple devices for yourself.

Working with a Magnetic Charging Pad

In chapter three, I described a special pad you can make and use to magnetize your drinking or plant water. If you'd rather not have a pipe standing in your refrigerator, you can use a magnetic charging pad. As used by some magicians, it consists of several magnets glued to a piece of wood. The completed assembly is usually covered with a silk cloth. The kind and strength of the magnets used are entirely at the discretion of the builder. I have seen these pads made with regular school-type bar magnets, as well as with ceramic magnets. Charms, written spells, and other things may be placed on the top of this pad, and left to temporarily bask in the magnetic field—usually overnight. Working something like an "Orgone accumulator pad," (which may be placed on top of the object on the magnetic charging pad if it is desired), the magnetic charging pad seems to add some non-physical energy to whatever is placed on top of it. See figure 8 and pages 41–42 for information on how to construct one.

These magnetic charging pads are often used to add a charge to powders or oils. Small quantities of powders may be put in a watch glass, or evaporating dish, which may be purchased at a scientific supply house. Oils may be placed in a bottle, and the bottle placed on the charging pad. Generally, I keep the material on the pad for about 30 minutes, although I have left materials on the pad overnight quite frequently, often by simply forgetting about them. The actual increase in the charge imparted to the powdered material does not seem to make a great deal of difference. I have come to believe that leaving the powdered material on the pad more than about an hour does not really increase the non-physical effect on the material very much at all.

Magnetically-charging oils and waters are a different matter. I prefer to place them in the refrigerator on the charging pad, or in the magnetizing pipe, for at least a week or so. This gives the water or oil the advantage of both the cold, which increases their ability to accept a charge, and the benefit of the magnetic field.

Protection with Magnets

A good friend of mine has set pairs of magnets at the front door of his apartment. Placed in a small hole he made in the plaster over his doorway, these short horseshoe magnets are fixed so that one of them points in, while the other one points out. Across the one pointing out to the hallway, he has fixed the sigil of a spirit that is protective in nature, to keep evil from entering his home. He simply glued this drawn sigil to the poles of the horseshoe magnet. Across the poles of the horseshoe magnet pointing into the apartment, my friend glued a copper sigil of Venus, to fill his apartment with beauty and comfort.

I must say that this is a process that I would never have thought of myself. My friend is quite pleased with it, attributing some positive changes in his life to his placing the magnets and sigils above his entry door. He mentioned to me that he had also heard of placing horseshoe magnets under the threshold of a home or store to attract customers to the business, and to bring good fortune to the home. That was the first time I had ever heard of anyone doing this, but magically, it does make sense. As I have said before, symbolism and intent are everything in magic.

My friend told me that the horseshoe above the doorway, found in many rural areas of this country and in Europe, is actually a magnetic charm, and it is the magnetism of the horseshoe that gives the charm its protective influence. I have never heard of this from anyone but him. I am skeptical of this effect, because if a horseshoe or any other suitable iron object is left in one place for a period of many years, it will certainly acquire some magnetism from Earth's own magnetic field; however, it's not a great deal of magnetic force, and even most toy magnets available today are a great deal more powerful than Earth's field at any particular point on Earth.

Magnetic People

This same friend is one of those people who can neither wear a watch nor use a computer. He has a great deal of personal magnetic energy, although not so much as to debilitate him from holding a rather ordinary job and working successfully in the world. However, he cannot handle computer disks, as his touch garbles their slight magnetic field, corrupting anything that is on the disk. On learning of this, his employer successfully placed him in a coordinating position, where he no longer has anything at all to do with computers.

One evening we attempted to find out if he could magnetize steel pins and sewing needles. Our conclusion was that he could not, although there are reports of people who have been able to do this just by rubbing a steel pin or needle with their finger. I have never seen this accomplished myself, but I have heard of it from two sources that I trust. I also understand that not too many years ago (in 1996, I believe) there was a television interview with a family that had the interesting affliction of being so magnetic that they could move iron pieces around, and could actually magnetize spoons and other objects.

All human beings apparently have a small magnetic organ inside the top of their nose. There was a book written some time ago about *The Magnet in Your Nose and Other Human Oddities*, but it has long passed from my memory just what this nose magnet is supposed to do for people. That many insects, birds, and other animals navigate using magnetic energy has long been recognized by biologists. In chapter 1, I mentioned research showing that monarch butterflies navigated by using Earth's magnetic field, among other navigational aids. Just how the birds and insects accomplish this is unknown to me, although I have read some of the research conducted by those who study animal migrations.

That some people are strongly magnetic in their own bodies is also a fact. These people usually cannot wear mechanical watches, and often they cannot wear the modern quartz crystal watches, either. Naturally, these people cannot use modern computers, as their very presence makes slush out of the codes on the magnetic media.

The late Al H. Morrison of New York City, one of the leading professional astrologers in the country, if not in the world, was another of the very few people I have known who was so afflicted. Out of respect for those who used computers, he would neither use their computers, nor even get too close to them. To the end of his life, he calculated all of his charts by hand, although many computer programs for astrologers were available at that time.

I have always found the subject of magnetic people interesting, although my opinion of what it may mean has greatly changed over the years. At one time, I believed that being strongly magnetic also indicated extrasensory abilities. I no longer believe that this is correct. Many people who have this magnetic quality or affliction—as the case may be—have no real extrasensory abilities at all. This is certainly an open door for further scientific research by some interested physician or medical researcher.

Incidentally, I myself cannot wear a mechanical watch for more than a week or so without having to send it to the jeweler to have it demagnetized. However, as far as I know, I have been successfully able to handle computer disks and even type on a computer from time to time without causing any catastrophic reaction. I do not use a computer to write as a matter of choice. The lovely IBM electric correcting typewriter that I do use is my pride and joy.

CHAPTER 5

The Lodestone Charm

As one of the favorite charms of the spiritual practitioner, the lodestone charm features prominently in folk magic. This charm is used to induce and maintain relationships, keep prosperity in the home, protect the home, and for a variety of other purposes, limited only by the desires of the person making the charm, or the requests made by the one using it. Beginning with a relatively small lodestone, the charm can grow over the years into a ball of magnetized iron filings as much as six or eight inches in diameter.

There are three parts to making and using these lodestone charms. Two of them seem to be common to all of the varieties of these charms that I have heard of. First is the process of making the charm itself, something that is usually accomplished by a spiritual practitioner for the one who will be using it. Second is the periodic ritual that is used to "feed" the lodestone charm. Third, and more rarely specified, is the ultimate means of disposition of the charm. Most of these lodestone charms are apparently meant to be kept forever. Naturally, there are an almost infinite number of variations possible within these three simple steps.

Making a Lodestone Charm

When a lodestone charm is made to gain or enhance a marriage, two lodestones are usually used. These lodestones should fit together fairly well, and they should be held tightly together by their mutual magnetic attraction. Obtaining two mating lodestones of this kind often requires a long and diligent search by the spiritual practitioner.[9] Most lodestone charms are made with only one lodestone, which is not nearly as difficult to find.

The lodestones, once obtained, are usually first cleansed of any influences that it may have gathered. This is accomplished by placing it under running cold water for a few moments. Sometimes it is placed in holy water for this purpose. Next, the lodestone is fed, by placing it in a small amount of alcoholic beverage—usually whiskey. After the lodestone has been in the whiskey a few moments, the spiritual practitioner prays over the glass containing both the whiskey and the lodestone, adding some of his or her spiritual power to the lodestone, and effectively telling the lodestone what it is to do. This is the "charging" of the lodestone, which if done while the lodestone is immersed in the alcoholic mixture, will have a somewhat greater effect.

The greater effect from charging a lodestone in whiskey or even in straight grain alcohol is due to the ease of charging alcohol itself. It is far easier to place a magical charge on alcohol than it is to place the same charge directly into any mineral or other solid. The lodestone may be left in the alcohol overnight if desired, to make the process of charging, or instructing it, even more effective. I recommend this practice, although I must admit that it is not always the one that I follow.

A dish, something like a saucer, or a small bowl, should be on hand in which to place the lodestone once it has been charged. The lodestone and its dish should also have some kind of cover. A new cotton handkerchief provides a good cover for most lodestones. The sole purpose of the cover is to keep dust and dirt off the lodestone. A solid cover is less desirable, as the lodestone is supposed to send its energy out into the world, attracting whatever the person owning it desires. Symbolically, using a solid cover over the lodestone would block this. In a few rare cases, usually for strong protective spells, or in the case of a business spell, an iron dish or even a small, cauldron-like iron pot is used to hold the lodestone.

The lodestone should now be presented to the person who is to use it. They should receive full instructions from the person who prepared it, telling them of the process for caring for their lodestone, and especially how they are to feed it each week, or each month, as has been arranged with the lodestone. It is always a good idea if a supply of magnetic sand or iron filings (they are the same thing), is given to the person at this time. By doing so, the person receiving the lodestone will have no excuse for not feeding and caring for their lodestone properly.

The lodestone is usually kept covered, and most often is hidden away. Placing the charm inside a kitchen cabinet or in the corner of a closet is usually advised. The charm is removed from its hiding place to be fed, but returned to it after the ritual of feeding is completed. This is as much to protect the lodestone from the gaze of those who might be envious of it, as it is to conceal the lodestone from the overly curious and inquisitive.

The feeding of the lodestone usually involves placing it in an alcoholic beverage. Whiskey is typically used for this purpose, although some practitioners prefer rum. The lodestone is placed in the whiskey for a short time, usually only about five to fifteen minutes. It is then returned to its dish, and a generous pinch of iron filings, magnetic sand, is sprinkled over the lodestone. The remaining whiskey is usually consumed by the person who is using the lodestone. When the lodestone is made for a couple, the couple usually shares the drink of whiskey between them.

In most cases, the lodestone is to be fed every week. Sometimes it is only to be fed monthly, and I have heard of one, made by a ceremonialist, that is fed only four times a year, on the equinoxes and solstices. Feeding the lodestone charm each week is far more common, regardless of the purpose for which it was made.

The ritual of feeding the lodestone is usually accomplished as I've described, but sometimes prayers are offered, and appellations (requests) to the lodestone are made at the time of its feeding. This seems to be more frequently the case when a lodestone is made to draw a specific thing to the person. These prayers are frequently offered to St. Iman, who, like St. Ajo, is a popularly constructed saint rather than a church-recognized saint. *Iman* means "lodestone" (or magnetic pole), and *Ajo* means "garlic." I seriously doubt that either of them are official saints of the Roman Catholic Church, at least I have never heard of either of them as being officially recognized as saints. However, the fact that the Church does not officially recognize them has nothing at all to do with the validity of the prayers being offered them. St. Christopher, who I understand is no longer recognized by the Church, is still a powerful saintly force in the universe.

What follows are some details of the various lodestone charms that I know about. There are many other spells and charms that I do not know about, so if your favorite is not listed, it is probably due to my ignorance of it.

A Lodestone Charm for a Specific Marriage

To gain a marriage with a specific person, the spiritual practitioner must first obtain a male and female lodestone, the male lodestone being one that has a convex part that fits as snugly as possible into the female lodestone's concave part. It is important that the two lodestones be held together firmly by their mutual magnetic attraction. The male lodestone is baptized in the name of the male by the usual process of the Christian baptism rite, or it is named in accordance with some other naming rite. The rite used is actually unimportant, as long as it pertains to either the practitioner or to the client in some way. The female lodestone is then baptized or named in the name of the female concerned, in the same manner. Ideally, the person receiving this charm, either male or female, has the lodestone baptized in their name first. This gives them precedence over the other person in the proposed relationship.

The lodestones may then be brought together, often using some of the words of the marriage ceremony. Again, the words and the ceremony used should be taken from some rite to which either the practitioner or the client relates. As the words declaring the couple married are being spoken, the lodestones are placed firmly together. The joined lodestones are then fed with alcohol—again, usually whiskey is used. As soon as the alcohol is added to the lodestones, the practitioner makes a prayer of blessing over them, usually one of the kinds of prayers used in blessing a marriage. The lodestones are then covered and left to rest in the alcoholic beverage overnight.

The following day, the lodestones are placed in their dish and may be given to the person who requested them. The lodestones are to be fed with whiskey or another specified alcoholic beverage every week. Once the desired marriage is consummated, the lodestones may continue to be fed by both parties, to insure a long, happy, and fruitful marriage.

The previous charm is most effective when there is a potential mate in sight, preferably one who is already dating the person that the lodestone is being made for. Obviously, making a lodestone charm for a marriage to someone whom you do not know, and especially someone that you have not yet met, is generally a waste of time. Once again, we are dealing with the sphere of availability. It is far better to stick with working for those things that are actually available to you, or to the person you are making a charm for, and to ignore those things that are not available to you. Otherwise, your successes are bound to be quite limited. A lodestone charm will not draw to you the movie star of your fondest dreams. It will, however, usually encourage your long-term but previously uncommitted lover to propose marriage to you.

A Lodestone for a Happy Marriage

This is for an already married couple. It is made from a matching pair of lodestones, exactly as was mentioned in the previous charm. The only difference is in the prayer that is made over the lodestones once they are put together. In this case, the prayer should be made that the marriage of the two people—refer to them by name—have particularly the qualities that the people want to have in their marriage, always including love, good health, increasing harmony, and increasing prosperity. If protection for the family is desired, it should be in the form of the lodestone attracting good spirits to protect the family, including all of its members. If properly made and fed as instructed, these lodestones can increase to a very large size over the years. Obviously, when the lodestones get so large that they cannot fit a glass for feeding, the feeding must be accomplished by pouring whiskey over the lodestone charm. Then the couple drinks what the lodestone does not adsorb.

A General Lodestone Charm for a Marriage

It is far more common for a woman to come to a spiritual practitioner with a request to find a husband because there is no one at all in sight for her. The first question that the spiritual practitioner must ask is whether she is taking advantage of her opportunities to socialize in an area where she can meet other people who are potential marriage partners for her. Once again, the sphere of availability comes into play. A woman living at home with her parents who does not socialize at all is unlikely to ever meet anyone who wants to marry her, unless it is by accident. Paying attention to this very important consideration will always enhance the success rate of the practitioner who makes these lodestones.

Aside from the always important, "Does she really wish to be married?"—a question that the practitioner must always silently ask the woman's innermost self— the next question to be asked is whether there are any impediments to her marriage. If she is committed to the care of her aging parents, or is otherwise blocked from marriage, including being blocked by overly restrictive religious beliefs, sexual problems, or parenting issues, it is going to be much more difficult for her to find a satisfactory mate. All of these questions obviously relate to the woman's personal sphere of availability. If it is found that her sphere of availability is too small, she should first expand what is available to her, by dating, changing her beliefs, going to a psychotherapist, or doing something in another way that will open up what is available to her. Talking with the woman will usually reveal ways in which her sphere of availability may be modified both favorably and successfully. If a person with a restricted sphere of availability is unwilling to work at modifying and enlarging it, making a charm for them is usually a complete waste of everyone's time.

All of those concerns aside, the lodestone charm for a marriage is made in much the same way as any other single-purpose lodestone charm. The only difference is that when the lodestone is charged, the prayer asks that it attract a suitable marriage partner to the person for whom it is being made. The name of the person for whom the lodestone charm is being made should be mentioned in the prayer, as well as any special conditions the person has indicated about their potential marriage partner. For instance, the person may require a partner who does not want children, or one who wants many children; a partner of a specific race, religious faith, or age; and so forth. This is why a great deal of information should be gathered first—to insure that the prayer is made in accordance with the person's actual desires. It is always easy to draw a mate to someone. It is more difficult to draw a *satisfactory* mate who will contribute to a permanent relationship or marriage.

Any lodestone charm made for a marriage should be fed each week until the lodestone has actually brought about the marriage. Feeding the lodestone should not stop with the engagement, as engagements have been broken in the past, and will be broken again in the future. Feeding the lodestone until the marriage has been both celebrated and consummated is always an excellent idea, and is to be strongly recommended upon giving the lodestone to the person for whom it has been made.

Once the marriage has been consummated, it is necessary to dispose of the lodestone because, unless its work is nullified, the lodestone will continue to try to draw another marriage partner. Obviously, this would be disruptive to the newly-formed marriage.

Having accomplished its purpose, the person should respect the lodestone as an instrument that assisted him or her in bringing about the marriage. Disposing the marriage lodestone is usually accomplished by taking it into the woods and giving it a "thank you" and a very liberal offering of alcoholic beverage poured over it before it is buried in the earth. I know of several successful marriage lodestones that have been buried in Central Park in New York City, but a rural woodland, or even a deep forest, is a better location.

A Prosperity Lodestone

As you have probably gathered by now, most of the variation in lodestones is in the prayer made over them when the lodestone is vivified, or brought to life, by the spiritual practitioner who makes the charm. This is also true of the prosperity lodestone. When praying for prosperity, the prayer made should be for increasing prosperity, continual supply, and some excess or surplus.

Praying for prosperity alone is too fundamental a level of prayer to allow the person to continually expand their economic evolution. This is why excess, surplus, or continually increasing prosperity must always be mentioned in the prayer. The eternally increasing cost of living must always be taken into consideration when the prayer is made. This is why asking for a specific amount of money each week is not a good idea. In the 1940s, someone who was making a hundred dollars a week was quite well off. Today, they would be classed as a pauper. Do not be afraid to ask for continual increase, and always avoid putting a cap on the amount for which you are praying. On the other hand, be aware of the sphere of availability, and be certain to ask for a level of prosperity that is actually available to the person for whom you are making the charm.

The person who requests such a prosperity lodestone should always be aware that they must continue to actively seek out economic expansion for themselves. They should not believe that the lodestone will do all of the work for them. As with any other magical charm, the lodestone will open opportunities, but it will not seize them for the person. The person who desires to profit from having such a charm must do his or her part as well. This means seeking out positions that are more profitable and studying, if necessary, to improve his or her skills for a better job with greater responsibility.

A Lodestone Money Charm for the Home

I wrote about this popular prosperity charm in my *Spiritual Worker's Spell Book*. It is certainly one of the most popular of the lodestone charms. It is also known as the Pot of Gold money spell. This spell is so popular that spiritual practitioners often make it up for their clients. This charm, although very well known among spiritual workers, was, to my knowledge, not written about until I included it in my *Spiritual Worker's Spell Book*. Naturally, every spiritual worker has his or her own variation of this spell, but the differences are minor, and usually unimportant. This spell has helped a great many people, which has given it its good reputation for being successful in assisting in the economic evolution of the home in which it is kept.

Two lodestones, one male and one female, as indicated by their shape, mutual attraction, and fitting tightly together, are used in this charm. The pair of lodestones is placed into a bowl, and the following is added:

- A teaspoon of iron filings, which are to "feed" the lodestones;

- A few of the gold and silver sprinkles or "sparkles" found in botanicas (herb and magic stores) and art supply stores. A dash of these sprinkles is quite enough—don't overdo it.

- Several grains of wheat, or the heads of three stalks of wheat, which still have the grains of wheat on them;

- Some copper, a copper disk or some copper coins, like a pre-1980 copper penny. Copper shavings are also good if you can find them.

- Five dimes; they do not have to be silver dimes, but if you have silver dimes, it would be good to use them.

- A few straight pins;

- Some grains of dried corn. Grains of hard corn or Indian corn are usually preferred.

- Something that reflects, like a small mirror from a purse-sized compact or some shiny sequins that can reflect an image. Some craft stores sell small round mirrors that are ideal for this.

- Three pieces of coral; red coral is thought to be the best, but white coral may also be used.

This assembly is prayed over, either by the spiritual practitioner or by the person making the charm for themselves. The prayer should include the name of the person the charm is being made for, and a statement that they should always have sufficient money in their life, as well as sufficient extra for entertainment and recreation so they may take pleasure in their life, as well as excess funds to put away for their old age.

The person receiving this charm is always instructed in its use. First, they must always keep this charm hidden away in a safe place so that no one else knows of it. It is not ever to be shown to anyone, and should not ever even be mentioned. They should take care to feed this charm only when they are alone, where no one can observe them. These precautions are necessary because the charm may be damaged by the unconscious envy or jealousy of another person to whom the owner might show it. This charm may even be harmed by the unexpressed or subconscious envy or jealousy of a mate.

On Tuesdays, the person for whom the charm was made takes the lodestones out of the bowl and puts them into a small glass of water that has had a teaspoon or so of whiskey added to it. The lodestones are allowed to sit in this water for about half an hour. Then they are to be taken out and prayed over by the person, who asks for the funds he or she believes will be needed in the coming week. Asking for an excess over what is strictly needed is considered a reasonable request. The lodestones are then placed back in the bowl, and some iron filings—about 1/4 teaspoon—are added to the bowl. The charm is then hidden away again.

The person may drink from the water that the lodestones have rested in. While drinking this water is usually considered a good idea, other practitioners do not recommend it. They believe that the water should be sprinkled around the house. Other practitioners believe in feeding the lodestone with straight whiskey, rather than water. If everything is going well with this charm, the lodestones will gradually grow in size. This is because the iron that you are using to feed them will stick and become attached to the lodestones over the passage of time.

A Protection Lodestone

After obtaining and cleansing the lodestone, the practitioner prays over the lodestone that it may draw good spirits to protect the one who needs protection. Protection from death, physical harm, accidents, as well as physical and verbal abuse should always be mentioned in the prayer. Specific protections from other people may be included, calling by name those who the person is to be protected against. It's important to make the prayer to attract good spirits, who are to provide the actual protection.

Sometimes these protection lodestone charms are put into small, iron, cauldron-like pots. I have never been able to find the reason for this, if there even is one. If you are inspired to place a protection lodestone into a small iron pot, or even into an iron metal pie or baking tin, which I have also seen, you should know that you certainly are not the first to do so.

I tend to put the lodestone charms I have made into those small clay dishes in which flowerpots are placed. Other workers use regular household dishes, saucers, and bowls. I have used these in the past as well. Either seems satisfactory to me. I believe that it is all just a matter of taste and whatever happens to be available to the spiritual practitioner at the time.

A Lodestone Charm to Obtain a Specific Thing

You can make a lodestone charm to obtain anything that the person who wants the lodestone desires. When this need is to be met on an ongoing basis, it is important to state that in the prayer. When I was living in a rent-controlled apartment, I once made a lodestone to insure regular heating oil deliveries, as I did not enjoy the heat failing in the winter when the landlord neglected to order oil. After enjoying reasonably good heat for three years, I discovered that the landlord was converting the building to gas heat. Naturally, at that point I had to get rid of the lodestone that I had made for regular oil deliveries.

As you can see, there is a certain amount of common sense involved in making lodestone charms. If you apply common sense to the charging prayer, you will certainly not go wrong in making up lodestones to suit your purposes, whatever they may be.

CHAPTER 6

Magnetic Spells

The Octagon Ring Magnet Spell

This spell involves the use of a special ring-shaped magnet, with about a 1 1/2" diameter and eight poles. These magnets are sold from time to time in military or electronic surplus stores. They are usually plainly marked with their characteristically odd eight-pole pattern of magnetism.

As there is some feeling among many people that the number eight deals with material success and the conquest of the physical world, I have seen these magnets made up into very nice charms that are used to attract good things to the one using them. The procedure seems to involve mounting these magnets on a backing of either copper or silver, and then inscribing in the center of the copper or silver what the person wishes to draw to themselves, or at least a symbol of the person's desires. I have seen two of these charms, and their wearers were quite happy with their effect, but I must admit that I have never made one myself.

My own tendency with such a magnet would be to write out what was desired and place the written request inside of the open center of the magnet. In this way, the force of the magnet would be applied to draw what had been requested to the one making the request. Of course, one of my reasons for doing the spell this way is that I am not adept in working with either copper or silver. Magic, however, is fundamentally a matter of symbolism and intent, and placing the written request inside of a circular magnet suits both the requirements of symbolism and intent. I believe this would work as well as making and wearing one of the more expensive silver or copper charms.

The Magnetic Wishing Cup

This spell, similar to the Octagon Ring Magnet Spell, involves a magnetic wishing cup, which at one time was sold by an occult and spiritual supply house in Brooklyn, New York. Making the cup is simplicity itself, should you desire to do so. You'll need:

- A piece of plastic tube or pipe, about 4" in diameter and about 1" high (or a bit taller than the magnets you are using);
- Eight small magnets;
- Glue or electrician's tape.

Glue the eight magnets around the outside of the piece of pipe; you could also use black electrician's tape to hold the magnets against the outside of the pipe. The magnets are arranged so that their poles are alternating: N - S - N - S - N - S - N - S. Finish it off with a cover and a base of wood, cardboard, or plastic.

To use the magnetic wishing cup, place a written statement of what is desired inside the cup, and allow it to sit there until the wish is fulfilled. As with most wishing cup spells, the results obtained from this one will also be quite variable. The results of these spells seem to depend a great deal on the person's ability to actually gain what it is they want from the universe.

I have also heard of people using this same cup to heal illness, by placing a trace of the person (a photograph, a lock of hair, or some other trace of the person) inside it. As this is also a wishing spell, I would not really consider the wishing cup to be a healing device, although in this case, the magnetic wishing cup is being used for absent healing. You may offer a prayer over the cup for the person's healing if desired.

The cup in the illustration was specially made by my magnetically-inclined student to hold several photographs of a friend's child who had been severely burned. The child recovered, although the hospital burn unit had originally held out little hope for him. This was not the only magical work done on the child's behalf, but in a case of this kind, I am certain that every little bit of assistance directed toward healing helps.

Meditation Aid Magnet

I previously mentioned placing a magnet on the forehead at the third-eye position when praying for a lover. In at least two instances, this procedure was able to draw a

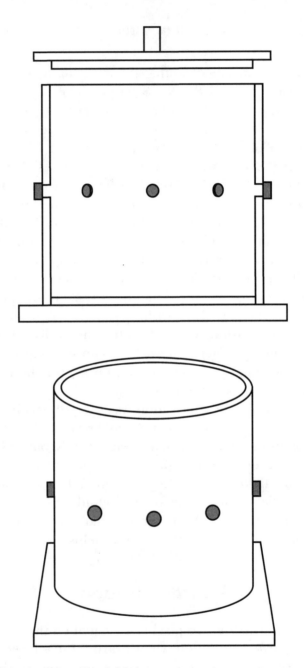

Fig. 11. A magnetic wishing cup

satisfactory lover to the person, and it had resulted in at least two marriages. I might add that there is another dimension to this procedure. According to several people who have tried meditating with a magnet on their forehead, they felt that placing the north pole of a magnet at this third-eye position seemed to increase the depth and value of their meditation. Naturally, this is a subjective perception, but if the person believes it to be helpful, it probably is.

One of the more difficult things in magical training is mastering the art of freeing the mind of extraneous influences. The mind's random thoughts and chatter are often so overwhelming that it is almost impossible to gain the calm, blank-mind state that the meditator desires. For many people, placing the north pole of a small disk magnet at the third-eye point in the center of the forehead seems to have the effect of muting, or even silencing, the chatter of the random, subconsciously-generated mental voice. This allows them to develop some gradually increasing stillness of the mind. Quieting the internal mental chatter slowly brings forth increasing clarity of thought in the meditator.

In this state of the empty mind, or the mind without thoughts, it is possible in prayer to request something from the universe with a greater degree of force, focus, and clarity, than would be otherwise possible. It is also possible to release those churning emotions and obstacles within you that block your own growth and self-knowledge. These obstacles continually come up into the mind, producing the "mind of a thousand thoughts." Of course, once you have reached this calm state in your daily life, you are not only more effective at any magical operation you may wish to pursue; you are also far more effective as a rational human being on the earth.

When using a magnet as a meditation aid or for any other type of self-development, it is important that you realize that once you have first achieved the state of the empty mind, you should immediately set the magnet aside. Now you must attempt to reach that same empty-mind state without the magnet's help. The magnet must not become a crutch; it must only be used as an aid to first reaching the state of the empty mind, and then only occasionally, and very infrequently, should you return to using it.

I have successfully recommended this procedure to those who want to master the art of mental concentration, which requires first reaching the state of the empty mind. However, I must again state that the magnet must be used only as an aid. When using a magnet or relying on any other external aid becomes a crutch, its true value is lost. There is a great deal of value in using aids to assist you in getting somewhere. There is no value at all in having to have a crutch to carry with you, as excess baggage, to attain an end that you can actually attain without using it.

Ceramic Magnets

These small magnets have a number of useful properties that transcend their more familiar use in holding notes to the refrigerator. As compact as they are, ceramic magnets are the most powerful magnets available. They may be used in a variety of spells. Because they are so powerful, they may be used to empower other charms, as well as used in places where magnets would not ordinarily be applied.

Some people place pictures of saints at their front door for protection of the home. In certain cases, they place small bags of "guinea pepper" (available at botanicas or herb stores) behind these pictures, to "feed the saints." Adding a small ceramic magnet to these little bags of guinea pepper increases the force of the saint and seems to make his or her presence in the home more powerful than it would otherwise be.

A Mexican woman who visited me one winter day recommended this novel use of a magnet. She noticed the picture of St. Jude that I have over my doorway, and suggested that I feed him with both guinea pepper and a magnet. Saint Jude and I are both quite happy with the result.

Using Magnets with Seals and Sigils

I have pointed out that seals and sigils glued to magnets seem to enhance the power of the spirit, or force, symbolized by the seal or sigil. This never seemed to be a particularly tricky operation to me; I had always thought that it was quite straightforward. I had been using this practice for several years when I happened to meet a demonolater, a person who worships demons.

This young man told me confidentially that he could greatly help me to enhance my practice of magic. Naturally, I was interested, as I am always interested in learning new things, as well as in perfecting myself in whatever area I already happen to know a little something about. He swore me to secrecy, and then proceeded to tell me about placing the sigil of a demonic spirit, as he called the Goetic entities, on a magnet. I showed him the magnets and seals that I had made and stored away in a cookie tin. He was crushed, yet he was honest enough to admit that the idea was not his. He had actually purchased the idea from someone else. I guess this idea is not as odd as I had once thought it was when I first began using it many years ago.

I began thinking of this process when I first became interested in using magnets in magical practice. Having had a number of pre-printed seals of Goetic spirits— the kind you can purchase from mail-order occult suppliers—I glued several of them to some circular magnets I had purchased at a surplus store. As these seals are about two inches square, I reduced a few of them on a photocopier at my neighborhood quick-printing facility to a bit over an inch square, so they would better fit the small magnets I had. I glued these seals to the north pole of the magnet, and awaited the results.

A friend who works with Rune magic suggested that I try this with a Rune charm, and he made one up for me. I glued it to a magnet. Although neither of us had ever heard of this process before, we both found that it worked quite satisfactorily. The seal with the magnet behind it is placed over a photograph of the person who is to have the energy of the spiritual force applied to them. Usually I just leave it there, held firmly in place on my metal storage shelf for a week or so. After that time I usually ask the person a question concerning their recent experiences and in most cases I receive a satisfactory answer. They usually tell me that their affairs are progressing, or that their problem has been resolved. This process is so much simpler than performing any kind of summoning operation, that I have practically abandoned summoning spirits altogether.

Can Spirits Use Magnetic Energy?

A friend of mine who practices necromancy, which deals with the spirits of the dead, told me that he happened to have a magnet lying on his dining room table which seemingly lost its magnetic power practically over night. He was not aware of this until he attempted to use it a day or two later. He noticed that at about the same time, one of the spirits he regularly works with had gained considerable strength and energy. He inquired of the spirit if it had taken energy from the magnet, but received at first a very ambiguous answer, and later a firm denial. He was not so sure that the spirit's denial was the correct response, and so he asked my opinion of the matter.

While I told him that I had never heard of such a thing, I asked around among my friends, as he inquired among his. Neither of us received an affirmative answer to the question from anyone we asked, as no one had heard of it before. Thus leaving me with the question in the heading above. Should the answer be affirmative in any way, I might only say that it would seem from the evidence that some spirits may be able to make use of magnetic energy to enhance their own vital energy.

Disk magnet

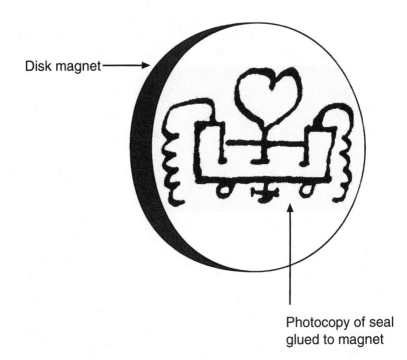

Photocopy of seal
glued to magnet

Fig. 12. A seal with a magnet. The seal shown here is for Vapula, who helps people in the handicraft professions and philosophy.

This was an isolated occurrence, and has not been repeated. It is a definite curiosity of mine, as I would certainly wonder at the method by which a nonphysical being can extract the magnetism from an alnico magnet. There are many odd things in the nonphysical world, but this is certainly one of the oddest things that I have ever encountered.

The fact that spirits whose seals and sigils are applied to magnets seem to feed on the magnetic energy has been mentioned earlier. This seems to apply to only certain Goetic spirits. The idea that this applies to the human dead as well is what gives me pause. Neither I nor any of my friends have ever heard of such a thing before this incident was brought to our attention. Should you happen to find a magnet that has suddenly lost its magnetism, you might consider this as one explanation for the sudden effect.

Christopher Hill's Magnetron Resonator

Mr. Hill is another investigator of odd effects, and many of his devices, magnetic and otherwise, are quite interesting. Should you come across any of his several books or monographs, they are well worth reading. He traces the origin of many of his devices back to either Atlantis or ancient Egypt (without any real reason to do so, in my opinion).

This device is used for healing by placing a trace of the person to be healed inside of it. My magnetically-inclined student made it for me, and while I have used it occasionally, I must admit that I have not had any remarkable results from it. My student made several of them, and our general consensus is that while they are interesting, they are certainly not as spectacular an aid to healing as Mr. Hill seemed to think that they are. Perhaps, as with several other things in this field, the result achieved depends greatly on who uses them.

Top view

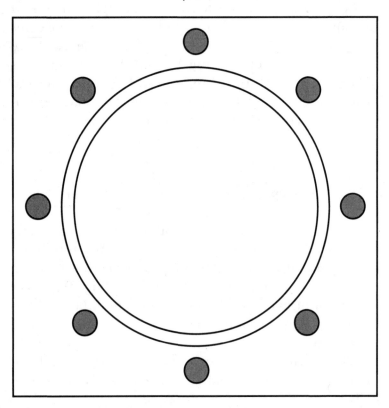

Side view

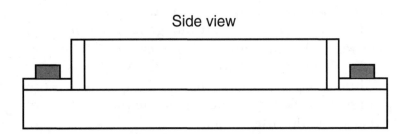

Fig. 13. Christopher Hill's Magnetron Resonator

CHAPTER 7

The Mesmer Board

The so-called Mesmer board was certainly not invented by Dr. Franz Anton Mesmer, although several of its various designs bear his name. Who actually originally developed what we now call the Mesmer board, and how it became refined into its many designs and styles, is one of those unexplained, and probably forever hidden, mysteries of the occult arts. The particular version of this device that I shall describe and explain in some detail is a design that a former student of mine made for me, and uses himself. He has told me that he did not originate the design, but obtained it from an acquaintance who also successfully experimented with these Mesmer boards. Those who have a natural affinity for working with lodestones and magnets seem to also have one for working successfully with such magnetic devices as Mesmer boards, energy rods, and even with magnetic healing. If you find that you have such an affinity, I sincerely encourage your further experimentation with these fascinating devices.

The Borderland Sciences Research Foundation, of Eureka, California published an interesting booklet titled *Vitic, or Magnetic Vitality*, which describes a somewhat similar mechanism. However, they credit the basic concept to the ancient Egyptians, something that I greatly doubt. This booklet covers material from various sources, including from séances. The information is dated from the late 1940s to at least the 1960s. Reprinted at various times, and in a number of editions, it is a very interesting work. My own edition is from about 1990. If you find you are interested in these magnetic devices, I strongly recommend that you purchase this fascinating booklet.

Borderland's version of the Vitic device is a vertical arrangement, which is apparently used primarily for therapeutic treatment. The Mesmer board with which I am most familiar is a horizontal version, and is used for stabilizing people's energy flows though the use of a magical trace or simulacrum. Aside from this, the circuitry, if I may call it that, is quite similar to the Vitic variety of Mesmer board.

The Mesmer board I am most familiar with (figure 14, p. 94) is made of two rectangular pieces of wood glued together, the smaller piece being the size of the photograph or the trace being used. Small bar magnets are placed along the narrow ends of the board holding the photograph or trace. These magnets present a magnetic field to the smaller board, which supposedly encourages the stability of the individual magnetic field of the person whose trace is placed on the smaller board. The larger board serves only to support the thin smaller board and the associated magnets. The completed board frequently also carries a Lakhovsky circuit (not shown in fig. 14), which is a coil of insulated copper wire left open at the ends. This coil is placed around the outside of the smaller board, supposedly increasing the effect of the magnetic circuit.

A piece of carbon placed on top of the trace or photograph and a central iron rod or steel focus (I have used a thumbtack) for the magnetic field complete the board. Alignment of the completed Mesmer board with the natural magnetic field of Earth supposedly assists in inducing greater stability of the aura of the individual whose trace is being exposed to the magnets on the board.

The principle of the Mesmer board's operation seems to be that at the approximate center of two attracting magnetic fields, there is located an iron or steel focus point, the action of which is further enhanced by a piece of hard carbon, which is placed over it, the photograph or trace of the person being between the two. This seems to place a flux of some kind on any living being whose trace or simulacrum is located at the junction of the iron focus point and the piece of carbon.

The piece of iron or steel in the center of the device does not seem to have, or to enhance, any of the properties of the magnetic field. The function of the piece of carbon seems only to delimit the magnetic fields, which in my opinion, are sufficiently far from the poles of the magnets to have only a very limited effect on either the iron or the carbon. The magnets used on these horizontal Mesmer boards have their poles on the ends, and are faced so that their opposite poles attract. However, as the field of any magnet is unique to that magnet alone, I do not believe that there can be any real interchange of magnetic energy between the two magnets. Therefore, despite much personal inquiry into the subject, I must admit that I have no idea at all how these devices operate.

Despite my lack of understanding how these devices work, I have heard remarkable testimonies from people whose simulacrums have been placed on one of these horizontal Mesmer boards. The most common report is an increase of vital energy, stamina, and a general increase in physical health. May this be due only to suggestion? If so, it is another case of the placebo effect. As far as I know, it may well be.

However, if these results are obtained only from the placebo effect, how is it possible to account for those cases where simulacrums have been placed on these Mesmer boards without the knowledge of the person concerned? A few of these people have also reported increased vitality, stamina, and health. Of course, the Mesmer board operations for these people weren't conducted in a double-blind test, so the favorable results that were obtained could be attributed to almost anything. The most obvious attribution, in my opinion, would be to the results of subconscious suggestion, and thus, once again, to the placebo effect.

The vertical Mesmer board, described in the *Vitic* publication, seems to have at least as many enthusiastic supporters as the horizontal one. I can only say that much like its horizontal cousin, its true operation is completely unknown to me, although I've heard many positive effects have been achieved with its use. The most common report is the temporary relief of chronic physical pain, which seems to last for as long as twelve hours after grasping the projecting iron rod for a few minutes.

The vertical Mesmer board, as illustrated by Borderland's *Vitic* device publication, is also to be used with a carbon rod to gain a longer-lasting effect. In figure 15, the resting place for the carbon rod is not shown, but it is located at the front edge of the device. (The photograph from which the illustration was made was taken without the rod in place.)

Figures 14 and 15 will give you some idea of the construction of these interesting devices. I encourage you to build one or both of these devices and experiment with them. They are, as far as I am aware, the two most common forms of the Mesmer board.

There is yet another device that is of a similar nature, although to my eyes it is more like the energy rods, mentioned in the next chapter. This device is also used to give energy to someone who is lacking in vital energy, and like the Mesmer board, it does seem to have this effect. It is a copper tube with a carbon rod inside, the point of which is aimed at a magnet that is positioned directly in line with it. A photograph or a simulacrum of the person to be energized is placed between the point of the carbon rod and the magnet. Figure 16 on page 96 shows the construction of this device.

A diagram of this device and an explanation of its use with a dowsing pendulum to indicate the subject's nerve force is to be found on page 38 of the 1990 edition of the Borderland Science Research Foundation's booklet *Vitic, or Magnetic Vitality.* The device shown above does not allow the carbon rod to be moved over a wide range, as the booklet suggests, and I have no understanding at all of how to identify one end of the carbon rod as being positive and the other end as negative, which is also mentioned in the description given in the *Vitic* booklet. However, in a dimly lit room, I have detected a reddish stream of nonphysical energy between the magnet and the carbon rod. I assume that it is this nonphysical energy, pass-

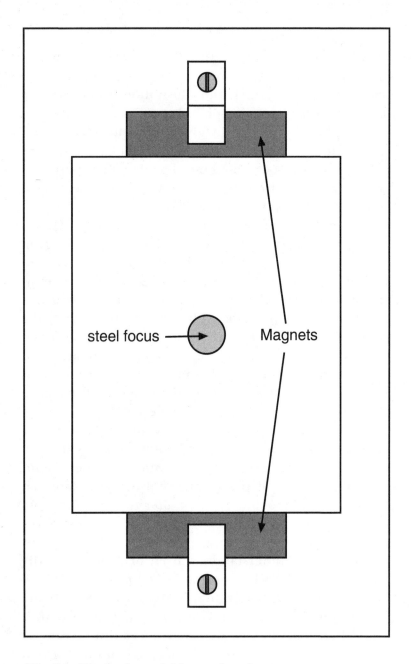

Fig. 14. The horizontal Mesmer board

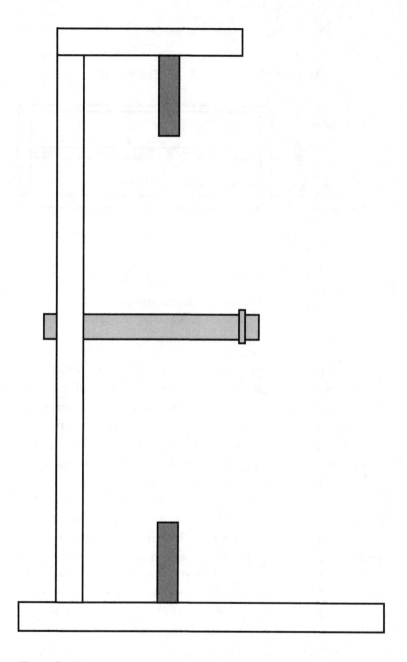

Fig. 15. The vertical Mesmer board or Vitic device

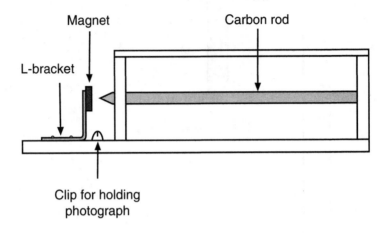

Magnet   Carbon rod

L-bracket

Clip for holding
photograph

Fig. 16. Energy rod & Mesmer board device

ing through the simulacrum, that adds vital energy to the individual represented thereon. I would hesitate to say that it enhances the individual's nerve force, or accomplishes anything physical at all. However, placing the simulacrum as described above does seem to result in the subject having more vitality and stamina.

Now, I am not aware if these devices have any real practical utility, or if they simply work through the ever-present force of suggestion, which obviously relates directly to the placebo effect. I would certainly not suggest using them in place of seeing a physician, and in fact, I always recommend that a physician be seen for any sign of physical disability or discomfort. There are many causes of physical discomfort, some of which have rather grave consequences if they are ignored for any time. Only a physician can accurately diagnose and treat an illness.

On the other hand, if you are interested in experimenting with these devices, they are reasonably simple to construct, and are not, to the best of my knowledge, at all dangerous to operate. I have had my own photograph placed for some time in a device of the third kind. I must say that I have felt no great effects from this, but I can attribute no harm to it, either. I still suffer from most of the many physical impairments of old age, so I must hasten to add that these devices are hardly to be considered a fountain of youth.

Multiple Mesmer boards of the horizontal style may be also made in order to hold a number of simulacrums of different people. This is a worthwhile project for someone who has a group of experimenters, or a number of people they want to treat in this way. These multiple boards are made in a manner quite similar to the single Mesmer boards. Figure 17 (p. 98) shows such a Mesmer board.

A useful simulacrum for the purpose of these Mesmer boards is a simple Polaroid photograph of the person. Polaroid photographs have the advantage of being both quite easy to take, and immediately applicable to the preconstructed Mesmer board. Furthermore, a Polaroid photograph is able to capture at least a part of the person's astral image, which is why I personally prefer to use them. An ordinary photograph, however, may also be used, and very little seems to be lost between the two.

If you want to use one of these horizontal Mesmer boards, I suggest that you place the photograph or simulacrum on the board for at least a month. In my experience, the longer the photograph is on the board, the better the results. I have had my own photograph on one of these devices for several years, and while I cannot

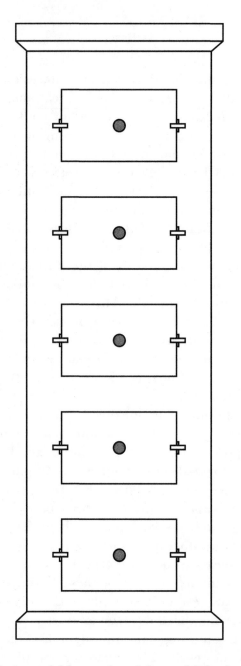

Fig. 17. Horizontal Mesmer board for multiple simulacrums

honestly say that I attribute any remarkable changes in my life to it, my energy flow seems to have evened out over this time. I might also add that about a month after my photograph was placed there, I began sleeping better at night, which may or may not have anything at all to do with the effect of the Mesmer board.

A fourth type of Mesmer board is also mentioned in the *Vitic* booklet. This one, supposedly given by the spirit of Anton Mesmer through a trance medium, is a horizontal variation on the vertical Vitic Mesmer board. The two horseshoe magnets are adjustable in their distance from the central iron rod, and there is a circle of copper wire outside the two magnets. It is supposed to be enhanced in its operation if the birthstone of the person being treated is attached to the tip of the iron rod. I have never seen one of this type, and have no interest at all in attempting to build one. Should you be interested in experimenting with one of these devices, a sketch of this device is given on page 27 of the *Vitic* booklet.

While these devices are interesting to experiment with, I have not been able to devise any kind of experiment that would tell me in an objective manner whether they actually have any real physical effect on the person who is using them. On the other hand, people have called me and asked to have me place their photograph on one of my "machines," when they have a particularly difficult task approaching them and feel that they will need the additional energy that the board will provide them. I do so, and they then seem content with their ability to work through their challenges.

Someone also suggested to me that a diamond would be a better form of carbon than the rods I have in my three rod type machines. This may very well be, but unfortunately, I do not have any diamonds. If you have one at your disposal, you might want to experiment with using it in this device. You might be able to make some interesting discoveries in this field. As with all of these various magnetic devices, there is still a great deal left to learn about these Mesmer boards.

CHAPTER 8

Energy Rods

Originating from the people at the Borderland Sciences Research Foundation, in their booklet *Vitic*, as well as from a number of more obscure references, the concept of energy rods is another idea that has been attributed by them and others to the ancient Egyptians.[10] While I seriously doubt the plausibility of the attribution, the practical effect of the application of these energy rods is of some interest in dealing with the occult effects of magnets.

The energy rods are supposed to be made of elemental carbon—which was once used in arc lights—and a permanent (rod or bar) magnet. (It's doubtful that the ancient Egyptians could have had access to either in sufficient form, or of the proper purity, to be nearly the same as what is described in the booklet). The Borderland Sciences Research Foundation booklet, *Vitic*, describes how to use the rods.

> If two rods are held, the carbon in the right hand, and the permanent magnet in the left, the effect [of "charging" the body of the person with vital nerve energy] is accentuated; but while the charge imparted

by the carbon endures for some twelve hours, that
exerted by the magnet ceases to be operative upon
relinquishment [of the magnet, by the subject].[11]

Earlier on, the author states:

Hard carbon such as is used in arc lamps will give
out a certain amount of force which experience has
taught us, is not to be distinguished from nerve
force. . . . If held in the right hand, it [the carbon
rod] produces . . . [a] positive deflection [on the
galvanometer], and [a] . . . negative if held in the
left hand.[12]

In the 1940s, at the request of the American Medical
Association, the Food and Drug Administration prohibited
the use of a sensitive galvanometer for medical diagnosis, ruling that it constituted medical fraud. All of the
known medical galvanometer instruments were seized by
the FDA at that time and destroyed. Some of the medical
practitioners who used them were even tried in court for
medical fraud. This nonintrusive method of obtaining a
very accurate diagnosis of certain physiological conditions, indicated by variations in the galvanic current at
different points of the human body, is almost completely
unknown today.

The fact that a galvanometric deflection is obtained
when a carbon rod is held in the hand is hardly convinc-
ing to those who look for a physiological or a chemical
change in the individual. The FDA investigators also
destroyed almost all of the research data and other literature concerning the galvanometer method of medical
diagnosis when they seized the equipment. The actual
information as to the details of measurement, and what

was actually being measured by the galvanometer deflection, is unavailable to anyone who might be interested in researching this process today.

I recall that certain cancers were located in their very early stages by means of the galvanometer. These cancers were then cured by another strange device, also attributed to the ancient Egyptians, called a chronoclast. I had a melanoma that suddenly appeared on my upper arm investigated and removed in this manner by a physician who used these devices in 1943. It has never reappeared, and I have never had another one. I believe that these odd medical devices, like several others in this rather exotic class, may well have been the victims of their own success.

Having said that, galvanometric deflections certainly meant something in terms of the physiology of the body. The occurrence of a positive deflection from a carbon rod in the right hand, compared with a negative deflection from a carbon rod in the left, meant that there was a potential method that magicians could use to strengthen or weaken a person. Since I was experimenting with magnets at the time that I read this in the booklet, I decided to look into this interesting effect.

I spoke to a client who was seriously afflicted with what used to be called "brain fag"—now generally known as nervous exhaustion—and we decided to attempt this method of therapy. I told my client that I had no idea at all if it would be successful, but that I thought it might at least be worth a try. I photographed my client holding her arms slightly out from her body, with hands open, and palms facing out. I took the picture with one of the original Polaroid cameras. When the photo was developed, I taped a pencil lead to the right hand and a magnetized sewing needle to the left hand in the photo. Scotch tape held these in place. As the effect was to continue only while the magnet and carbon were being "held" in her hands, I then placed the photograph into an envelope and put it in her file.

The client said that she felt no immediate effect, but considering the weak nature of the client's non-physical perceptions, with which I was passingly familiar, I was not at all surprised. I asked her to return in a week, at which time she informed me that she felt much better. She told me at that time she no longer felt so overwhelmed by the circumstances of her life. In another month she was back to being on a more or less even keel. I left the photo as I had made it up in her file for another month or two, at which time I removed the pencil lead and the magnetized needle. Apparently, that had cured the condition, as my client never complained of it again, although I saw her at least once or twice a year for several years after that incident.

This success emboldened me to attempt another experiment, this one of a somewhat perverse nature. When one of my students complained to me about being placed in a very negative position by a coworker, I decided to do something to assist him. He had a photograph of the person who was harming him that had been taken at a company Christmas party. Although not posed as accurately as the one I had purposely taken of my client, I judged it sufficient for the purpose at hand. I then arranged a magnetized needle on the person's right hand, and a pencil lead on their left hand. A week later, my student told me that the person seemed to be disoriented, and losing vitality. At least the person was no longer attacking my student, which was the benefit that I had sought. I left the needle and lead in place only a week in this case. Later on, when the person went back to verbally attacking my student at work, I replaced the pencil lead and needle on the photograph for two weeks, with the same excellent results. The individual had apparently learned their lesson, as their verbal attacks and negative critical comments concerning my student stopped permanently.

As far as the healing effects of physically holding a carbon rod in one hand and a magnet in the other are concerned, I have felt this myself. I have a carbon welder's cutting rod, which is a solid piece of carbon about a half inch in diameter and a foot long. I have found that holding this rod in my right hand and placing my left hand on a magnetic charging pad is quite effective in helping me rejuvenate when I am tired. I combine this with taking four slow, deep breaths, and I must admit that it makes me feel better than just taking four deep breaths alone. I have also recommended this procedure to several of my magically-inclined friends and many of my former students. They tell me that they have found it to be quite useful, as well.

I do not recommend this procedure as a panacea or for the healing of any condition, but I do recommend it as a way to refresh yourself when you feel tired, as after a day's hard work. It does seem to have a calming and balancing effect. I do not have a magnetic rod of the kind recommended for the left hand, but a friend has one and he says it is ideal for the purpose. Having tried it, I would say that it does enhance the effect. I suppose that an ordinary bar magnet would probably suffice, making the use of a special magnetic rod unnecessary.

Obviously, the effects of these devices are entirely subjective. I have had clients who looked a bit frazzled hold the carbon rod in their right hand, and they have told me that they felt no effects from it at all. Yet, at the same time, I saw their aura become less disjointed—more solid—even as they were telling me that it was having no effect on them. Those who are more sensitive to the nonphysical universe will probably notice greater effects from these magnetic devices, as well as from many other things, than those who are not as sensitive.

A Magnetic Magic Wand

I also have one of these carbon rods in a copper tube that has a small but powerful ceramic magnet placed at one end of the carbon rod. This rod seems to have an interesting effect when it is used as an instrument to dispel thought phantoms around a person. I use the rod to carefully sweep from the left side of the person's head, up over their crown, then down the right side of their head. I then sweep in the same way from their face and down over the back of their head to the shoulders. While it is certainly not as cleansing as a full spiritual cleansing, it is quite beneficial in its effects for those who tend to live in a fantasy world.

My magnetically-inclined former student made up this wand for me. I was amazed when a ceremonial magician I know said that it was the most powerful magic wand he had ever seen. He was highly impressed by the intrinsic power he sensed in it. I sent him on to my former student, who made one up for him, to his great delight.

Fig. 18. A mechanical magic wand

I truly doubt that any of these devices originated in ancient Egypt, or that they were actually the inventions of Dr. Mesmer. However, the origin of these rods is not a real concern of mine; I am only interested in their effect on people. It is quite common, especially in the occult community, to attribute inventions to famous persons or to unknown or barely heard of, even mythical, ancient societies of some kind, who have themselves probably never heard of them. It gives these inventions a certain cachet in the eyes of those who use them and those upon whom they are to be used. Can we also say that it enhances the placebo effect, by suggesting to the user that these devices will actually perform miracles? I really believe we can.

CHAPTER 9

Distant Communication: Sending a Covert Message

One of the more interesting applications of magnetic energy is to send a covert message to another person. The method of communicating this message, as described below, may be made completely automatic. Once the equipment is arranged, and the message established, the equipment may be left to operate by itself, completely unattended, for as long as you desire. The message is transferred from the tape of an ordinary tape recorder to the person's subconscious mind, through the intermediary of a Polaroid or other photograph. The person receiving the covert message does not hear "voices in their head," nor do they have any other conscious awareness that they are continuously receiving the nonphysical impression of the information that you desire to impart to them.

The primary disadvantage of this method is that a single brief message must be carefully prepared, and sent to the person continuously for a period of at least a month. It is greatly preferable if it is continuously sent to them for several months, or even longer. This process may not be used for communicating messages that require action, especially those that require any kind of immediate action. It may only be used for those messages that involve a gradual change in the person's belief concerning himself or herself, something else, or someone else. Like gentle drops of water, which in time will wear away the hardest stone, the subconscious reception of the message will gradually convince the person to change, or to modify their beliefs concerning the information placed within the message being continuously sent to them.

On the other hand, it appears that there are some people who are sufficiently out of touch with themselves that it is impossible for them to be able to receive any message that is not transmitted to them in a very physical manner. Because of this, it is necessary to carefully select the person to whom you wish to transmit this kind of message. Should you pick someone who cannot receive this message, or someone who will completely block its conscious reception, you are wasting your time trying to send the message to them.

By literally surrounding the person with the message being sent them, the sensitive person's own subconscious mind will eventually supply all of the rationalization and justifications necessary for their gradually changing belief. Thus it is not necessary in the message to explain the why of the matter, it is only necessary to state what you wish them to accomplish. Of course, the more difficult the change is for the person to accept, the longer time the message instructing them to change their beliefs must be sent to them. In some cases, it may prove impossible for them to ever accept the idea of the change you are asking them to make. This is one of the many disadvantages of this interesting method of subtle communications.

Another disadvantage of this method is that while people may very well be subconsciously persuaded of something, getting them to consciously act on, or even to consciously accept, any of the many contradictory and confusing subconscious messages and beliefs that any given person may hold in their mind at any time, is considerably more difficult. This is why it is always best when using this method to create a message that will enhance, reinforce, and possibly expand, any personal belief that the person may already hold deep within themselves.

Messages must always be both short and positive. They should be the same as the commands phrased as suggestions that are given in hypnotherapy. The message being transmitted to the subject should be phrased in the form of brief positive statements, rather than being sent as either commands, suggestions, or gentle requests. The following unemotional statements are examples of the kind of message that seems to work best with this method:

Your mathematical abilities are increasing.
You enjoy mathematics.
You understand mathematical equations.

Or

You no longer enjoy smoking.
You no longer enjoy drinking.

The process of transmitting the subtle message is accomplished by taking a small loudspeaker and fixing the voice coil, the center moving part of the loudspeaker, with some strong glue so that it no longer moves. Hooking up the output signal of a tape recorder to the loudspeaker will now cause the magnetic field of the magnet that is in the center of the loudspeaker to be modulated or changed slightly by the message being played on the tape recorder. This happens because as the voice coil can no longer move, it must modulate the magnetic field of the permanent magnet instead.

By placing a photograph with a thin piece of iron attached to the back directly over the magnet and coil of the loudspeaker, the message from the tape recorder will be transmitted indirectly to the person through the means of their photograph. The message to be sent should be recorded on one of those repeating tapes—the shorter the better—such as those used in answering machines and to make announcements in stores. I first used a three-minute tape, but eventually I found one-minute tapes, which proved to be far better for the purpose. These tapes are usually available at stores specializing in audiovisual equipment. They are only slightly more expensive than ordinary cassette tapes.

When someone has a grievous social disability, such as alcoholism, this is one way to gradually and slowly convince him or her that they should seek to put an end to their affliction. Admittedly, it is a slow process, and not at all a certain one, but in some cases I believe that it is worthwhile to attempt this process, to produce the change in the person's behavior. I have had some slight success with this method, although I must admit that it took six months to gain my first quite moderate success. There are probably other and faster methods to gain these ends, but there is no other method that I know of that is so covert.

An illustration of a device of this nature is in figure 19 on page 113. It is made from a wooden base, which holds the small loudspeaker, and a back plate to hold the photograph. To obtain the best effect, the photograph

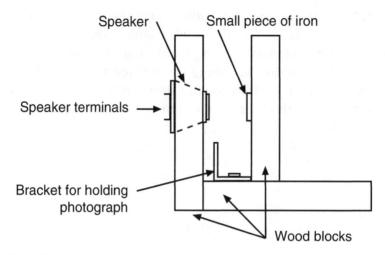

Fig. 19. Covert communications device

should be as close to the voice coil of the loudspeaker as is physically possible.

This is another home workshop project that may be made in a few hours. The longest part of the project is the time required for the glue on the voice coil to dry. It is an interesting device, and along with the repeating cassette and the tape recorder, it can be placed completely out of sight, where it is left to do its work automatically . while you go about your usual routine unhindered by other considerations.

Remember: don't expect this device to produce results in every case, or to produce the kind of results you expect in a short time. If you decide to make one and use it, I suggest that you allow at least six months for it to have any noticeable effect on your first subject. Even then, it may not be as strong an effect as you might desire. Those few people who are actually in touch with their subconscious mind will notice the change in their thought processes more rapidly. Unfortunately, they are also more able to turn away from these changes in belief, knowing that they are being transmitted to them from an external source. However, this device offers an interesting technique, which has some limited uses in therapy.

CHAPTER 10

Magnetic Healing

One of the more enthusiastic exponents of an alternative form of healing once said, "If this is true, then all medicine is false." Obviously there is not much that may be said in favor of that kind of emotionally driven statement. As it is with many other things, there is much that is true, and there is much that is false in any artistic technical modality, whether it is sculpture, healing, art, or poetry. The problem we find here is that there is never just one solution to any given problem. Oftentimes, there is not even just one best solution to the given problem. We must bear this in mind when we look into the many methods of healing which are used, or which may have been used, through the ages.

Once we truly understand that an enthusiastic and believing doctor, prescribing a placebo to a needy and believing patient, will perfectly cure that patient no less than 30% of the time, we have lost the right to criticize any healing modality, no matter how odd it may seem, or how insulting it may be to our sense of propriety. We must always look at healing modalities in terms of what is accepted and believed by both the patient and the prescriber at the time. We should also be aware that those things that are said to be new always tend to hold more favor with the patient than those treatments that are tried and true in the eyes of the medical professional. While advancement in healing the ill may change at a rapid pace, most medical professionals will maintain a firm and practically unquestioning belief in what they learned in medical school throughout their entire career in medical practice.

In a rather odd book concerning his travels in the Amazon River basin,[13] a Philadelphia dentist described witnessing a native shaman, or witch doctor, extract a worm from his guide's mouth. The guide had complained of a badly infected tooth, and the dentist had admitted to him that without his medicines and instruments he could do nothing for him. Not only did the infection go down once the worm was removed, the tooth healed so completely that after just one week, the dentist could find neither cavity nor abscess in or around the tooth. Now, according to modern dentistry, that is just not supposed to happen. According to the dentist, who was amazed by witnessing it, it did. Can we credit this kind of healing to the placebo effect, the strong and focused belief of the person whose tooth was so healed? I really do believe that we can.

Those who have spent time working with the invisible forces of the universe can well understand that such a cure is actually possible. As recent psychological research has found, one of the most important contributions to healing any illness is the rapport that exists between physician and patient. This is why those physicians who have developed a better bedside manner are generally more successful in their healing efforts than those who have not. Many patients report that they feel better just being in the presence of their favorite physician. Those who do feel this way are already on the road to health, almost regardless of what therapy the physician may prescribe for them.

The psychological component present in all physical healing does not go completely unrecognized by the medical profession today. The purpose of the double-blind study in accepting new medications is to weed out the influence of the placebo and the ever-present force of suggestion. In a double-blind study, neither the prescribing physician nor the patient knows who is receiving the medicine and who is receiving the identical placebo. Thus, the only unrecognized feature is the charismatic bond between the individual patient and the individual physician, which our objective rational science has found no way to measure yet.

I mentioned previously that as far as I know there have been no double-blind studies of the therapeutic effects of magnets on human illnesses.[14] I have no idea as to how one would be conducted, as the design of medical experiments is very far from my quite limited field of knowledge. However, until there has been some objective proof of the effectiveness of magnets in the practice of healing, I will not advocate their use. On the other hand, there's no stopping those who may wish to experiment on themselves in this field. Having said that, here are a few of the therapeutic remedies that I have heard advocated by others for the application of magnets:

- Supposedly, broken limbs that are exposed to a constant magnetic field heal faster than those left without such exposure.

- Magnets have been used to relieve pain. Dr. Julian Whitaker enthusiastically claims that they may be used to gain remission for all kinds of pain. The bibliography of his book, *The Pain Relief Breakthrough*, gives a great number of studies of magnets and pain, but I see none there that are truly peer-reviewed double-blind studies, published in professional medical journals. This is something that I believe would lend greater credence to the work, but that is my own opinion.

- Doctors at the University of Regensburg, Germany, have conducted a study using a technique called high-frequency repetitive transcranial magnetic stimulation (TMS) to help smokers who wish to quit cigarettes. The technique involved the transmission of pulses of magnetic energy transmitted via a coil-shaped stimulator placed on the head. Each subject in the study underwent two trials of active stimulation and two of "sham" stimulation on four consecutive days, without knowing which was which. The subjects smoked significantly fewer cigarettes during the 6-hour period following the active treatment compared with the sham treatment. The doctors are further researching the effectiveness of the treatment as an alternative to conventional drug-related methods for treating other addictions as well.[15]

- TMS is also being studied by Harvard researchers at McLean Hospital in Belmont, Massachusetts, as a method for treating depression, mania, posttraumatic stress disorder, Parkinson's disease, and obsessive-compulsive disorder.[16]

- Magnets have been used in minor surgery to correct a birth defect known as esophageal atresia in which the upper and lower halves of the esophagus are not connected as they should be. Dr. Mario Zaritzky and colleagues from the Sor María Ludovica Hospital in La Plata, Argentina, successfully corrected the defect in five patients. One magnet is placed through the mouth into the upper part of the esophagus and then, through a small hole made in the stomach, a similar magnet is put into the lower part of the esophagus. The attraction of the two magnets eventually pulls the disconnected parts of the esophagus together.[17]

The Japanese have done a great deal of research concerning magnets and illnesses, as have some Indian researchers. Again, none of them seem to have met the test for an objective peer-reviewed double-blind study. Because of their research, several Japanese companies sell magnetic amulets, bracelets, and even small self-adhesive spot magnets. Some of these items have been imported into the United States, while others have not. However, as a result of their manufacture in Japan, several American companies have also begun manufacturing a number of these interesting magnetic devices.

I suppose that the best thing I can say in this subject is that if you wish to use magnets to heal any condition, I urge you to exercise caution. See your physician for treatment first, and use magnets only as a supplement to the regular process of healing. You may find that magnets are effective, or you may not.

If you are healthy, and in good physical condition, you can perform a number of interesting experiments with magnets that are said to increase your strength and vitality. You should treat these things as the experiments that they are. You should never attempt to treat any physical or health conditions with them. In addition, should you believe for any reason that any of these experiments have even the very slightest negative effect on you, you should discontinue that experiment immediately.

There is at least one reasonably safe way of experimenting with magnets in nonphysical healing. This is by using a horseshoe magnet to clean a person's aura.

Magnetic Aura Cleansing

Cleaning and balancing the aura seems to be one of the major preoccupations with many of the people in the eclectic New Age movement. One of the local New Age newspapers lists at least a half dozen practitioners of the art of aura cleaning, balancing, and revitalizing. While treating the aura with crystals is one of the latest fads, it should come as no surprise to anyone that there is also a way to clean and balance the aura with a magnet. I have had this method used on me, and I have also used this method on others. Whether or not you think that it works for you depends on whether you subjectively think that you feel any better after it has been done to you. It is, in my own opinion, at least as effective as having my aura cleaned and balanced with a collection of artistically arranged crystals, which another friend did for me one evening.

To use a magnet to clean and balance your aura you will need a fairly strong horseshoe magnet, and about six inches of cotton string. My local automobile supply store sold me the horseshoe magnet, and I got the string from the wrapping of a package from a retail store. Tie string around the curve of the magnet, and tie a knot in the string about six inches from the point where it is tied to the magnet. This makes it easier to hold and swing the magnet by the string.

Now have your friend and fellow experimenter lie face down, either on a table or on the floor. Holding it by the knot in the string and about an inch or two above their left leg, begin moving the magnet slowly up their leg. When the magnet decides to swing across their leg, or to gyrate in a circle, keep it there, allowing it to swing by itself until it stops. When the magnet is still, you should resume moving it slowly up their leg, stopping whenever the magnet swings across the leg or gyrates in any way. Once you have covered the entire left leg to the hip, you must return to just below the right leg and repeat the performance. When you have done both legs, you should then begin at just below the juncture of the legs at the pelvis, and proceed in the same way up the trunk and the spine. You will end up with the magnet just over the top of the person's head.

Usually this is enough of a treatment for your friend, as lying in that position for any length of time can be enough of an effort for an evening, especially for those of us who are elderly. If you want to, you can change places with the person you worked on, and let them clear your aura. If they are still game, and if you are also up to it, you can have them lie on their back and repeat the same procedure on their front. At this point, you can also do their arms after you finish with the head, starting at the fingertips and moving to the shoulder.

If you feel that this treatment has benefited either you or your friend, it should be repeated, as one magnetic aura treatment is not intended to have any long-term or permanent effect. Weekly treatments for at least the first month are recommended for restoring and maintaining balance in the aura. In cases where the aura has been badly distorted, or even had its polarity reversed (which rarely ever happens), a treatment three times a week is usually recommended for at least the first month, followed by once-a-week treatments for another month or so. This is a somewhat similar schedule to what the crystal treatment people recommend. It is important that you realize that all of these alternative therapies usually take a great deal of time to accomplish anything that will have any physical effect at all. You should not expect to receive any physical healing from this aura cleansing procedure.

When performing this aura cleansing and rebalancing, some people say that holding a carbon rod about six or eight inches long in the right hand makes the treatment more effective. This is similar to the procedure mentioned in chapter 8. I have tried the aura cleansing both ways,

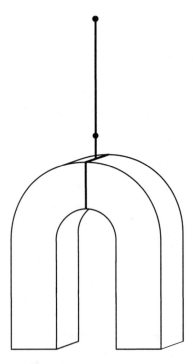

Fig. 20. An aura-cleansing magnet

and I personally noticed no difference. But then I may just be insensitive to the subtle differences involved.

If a bar magnet is suspended so that one pole is pointing down, and passed over another person about an inch or less from their bare skin, it is sometimes found that the person can feel a slight tingle of energy from the magnet. The occasional person who is sensitive enough to feel the slight tingle of magnetic energy is what probably gives the magnetic effect its reputation for healing.

Kilner, the hospital electrician who wrote a book on the human aura,[18] used electromagnets to distort the human aura.

He discovered that the human aura could be distorted by the proximity of an electromagnetic field. He practically ceased his experimentation with electromagnets when he found that the same effects could be achieved using verbal suggestion. A few magnetic healing experimenters today use electromagnetic fields in their work; others find that the constant energy of the stronger permanent magnets available today give more uniform results. Perhaps Kilner's discovery that suggestion is a substitute for the energy of magnets is the real reason why magnets obtain the effects that they do. It may also explain why magnetic healing seems to operate so slowly, as it proceeds from the nonphysical aura to the physical body.

Magnetic Shoes

Placing small disk magnets, with the north pole facing up, in your shoes is said to assist you in gaining strength and endurance. I experimented with this, using a pair of thin disk magnets about a half-inch in diameter. I wore the two magnets in my shoes for a whole day. While I did not notice any surges of energy, I did not get particularly tired either. It was actually a very normal day for me.

I did notice a sensation, very much like walking with stones in my shoes, which disappeared when I removed the magnets at the end of the day. I would recommend this as a safe experiment to try, as it just possibly may have some useful effect for you. Later in my experimenting I placed the two disk magnets under a shoe insert, or shoe liner, made of lambs' wool. I wore the magnets in this manner for a few days. The lambs' wool shoe inserts eliminated the stone-in-the-shoe feeling, and I did have a few good days. It would be quite hard to say that the magnets were responsible for my feeling good, however.

It could have just as well been my biorhythms, my horoscope, or almost anything else.

Treating Physical Conditions with a Magnet

With this in mind, the following information reveals what the two poles of the magnet are supposed to do, at least as far as physical healing is concerned. . .

The south-pointing pole is said to have the qualities of assisting recuperation and recovery. It is said to shrink tumors and arrest the growth of everything from microorganisms to cancer. It is used to help the body fight infection and increase the healing process. Applying the south pole over the heart is said to slow the heart function. It is also said to increase the life span, draw oxygen, and maintain the balance between the energy fields of the body. It is also said to stop pain and reduce the calcium deposits that are responsible for arthritic joints. Thus, the south-pointing pole of the magnet is generally applied directly onto the body, and held in place with adhesive tape or the like.

The north-pointing pole is said to activate and stimulate. It works in an opposite manner from the south pole, increasing infection instead of reducing it, and decreasing the life span instead of increasing it. Supposedly, applying the north pole to a cancer would increase the spread of cancer, instead of limiting it.

It would seem that a great deal of experimentation would be required to actually prove the validity of any of these statements. I certainly would not place a great deal of faith in them. I seriously doubt that I shall see any kind of magnetic healing approved by the FDA in my lifetime.

Appendix
The Adventures of
Dr. Mesmer

Franz Friedrich Anton Mesmer was born on May 23, 1734 in Iznang, Swabia, on Lake Constance, a part of Germany. He was the son of a forest warden, or game-keeper, to the Bishop of Constance. When he was nine years old, he entered a local monastery school, where, when he was fifteen, he won a scholarship to the school at Dillingen. An excellent student, he entered the Jesuit University of Ingolstadt, Bavaria at eighteen, in 1752. Less than twenty-five years later, Adam Weishaupt would be appointed professor of canon law there, and in 1776, Weishaupt would found his Society of Bavarian Illuminati, which would become the hallmark of secret societies the world over.

At Ingolstadt, Mesmer studied the works of Paracelsus, and obtained the degree of Doctor of Philosophy. He then traveled to Vienna, where he briefly studied law. Highly impressed by the works of Paracelsus, and wishing to become a physician, he began the study of medicine under the famous Dr. van Swieten of the medical faculty at the University of Vienna in 1760. At that time, the University of Vienna was one of the leading medical institutions of Europe.

On May 27, 1766, Mesmer received his medical degree. He was 32 years old, a late age to become a physician at the time. Dr. Mesmer believed that the tide-like motion of a magnetic fluid, which he called "Gravitas," within the human body, was what produced vitality and physical health. He further believed that the heavenly bodies of the solar system, and even those of the stars in the universe beyond, affected the flow of this fluid within all human and animal bodies. In his eighteen-page dissertation at the University of Vienna, "The Influence of the Planets on the Human Body," he borrowed heavily from the works of both Newton, whose theory of gravity was reasonably new, and of the British physician Richard Mead, who had earlier put forth much the same argument.

Dr. Mesmer soon married a wealthy and aristocratic widow who was ten years older than he. His marriage gave him solid connections to the aristocracy of Vienna, among whom he soon built a prosperous medical practice. He was quite active, both socially and medically, and was soon doing very well in both spheres.

Mesmer, who was fond of music and skilled at both the pianoforte and the cello, soon turned his Vienna home into a musical venue. Hayden, Mozart, and Mozart's father became both his frequent visitors and friends. Mozart's first opera, written when he was only twelve, was first performed at Mesmer's home. Later on, Mozart placed a small tribute to his friendship with Dr. Mesmer in his opera, *Cosi fan Tutte*, in which he had one of the characters heal an ill person by using magnets.

In 1774, Mesmer became interested in the magnetic healing theories of the Austrian royal astrologer, Father Maximilian Hell. At that time, Father Hell was professor of astronomy at the University of Vienna. Father Hell had used iron and steel magnets of various shapes, made to suit the part of the body to which they were to be applied, to successfully treat a variety of illnesses. After either speaking with, or studying with, the well-known priest (the accounts vary), Mesmer began practicing magnetic healing with his own patients. He was immediately successful in this venture as well.

Mesmer was also influenced by another priest, Father Gassner, who successfully used what he called "magnetic passes," along with the laying on of hands, to successfully treat members of his parish, as well as several outsiders. These magnetic passes eventually were aped into the stuff of grade-B horror movies, but at the time, they seemed to have produced some real results in those people whom the sincere priest treated.

With the information gathered from these sources, Mesmer began to "magnetize." He magnetized his patients' drinking and bath water, their clothing, and other physical objects. Aside from using iron magnets as a treatment device, he also magnetized by making dramatic passes with his hands, just as Father Gassner had done. Mesmer's success was immediate. He had many reported cures from his magnetizing efforts, and the Augsburg Academy even reported that Dr. Mesmer had discovered a new force in the universe.

Mesmer was then called upon to treat a seventeen-year-old girl, Franzl Oesterlin, a relative of his wife, who was suffering from a variable condition, which apparently included symptoms similar to hyperventilation. The application of magnets to her body caused her to enter into a crisis. This was followed by a dramatic improvement, and gradually led to a full remission of her debilitating physical condition. Franzl eventually made a complete recovery, married, and had children. Naturally, this remarkable cure only increased Mesmer's fame. He was soon traveling around Swabia, Bavaria, Switzerland, and as far as Hungary, treating both the aristocracy and the socially well-connected.

Mesmer was then called upon to treat Maria Theresa Paradies, who had been blind from the age of three, but who had learned to play the piano professionally. Mesmer was successful in partially restoring the girl's sight, but was then forcibly forbidden by her father, sword in hand, from treating her any further. A blind female pianist was quite a novelty at the time; a normal girl who could play the piano would not draw a paying crowd, even though she played quite professionally. The girl's father accused Mesmer of seducing the girl, although he had been in the same room with them whenever Mesmer had treated her. The conflict between her father and Mesmer caused the girl to relapse, and her blindness swiftly returned. Although she remained a satisfactory piano player, she was blind for the rest of her life.

The girl's father complained about Mesmer to the Viennese medical council, and the medical council, which had been looking for any excuse to rid themselves of Mesmer's fierce competition, quickly appealed to the crown. At the formal and stern request of the royal medical council, the Empress of Austria banished Dr. Mesmer as a fraud and an impostor. He left Vienna, moving on to Paris, where he arrived in February 1778. Finding no great immediate reception in Paris, he set up his clinic in nearby suburban Créteil.

Initially, Mesmer was successful in Paris, receiving the patronage of Marie Antoinette and much of the nobility. However, he was opposed in his practice of magnetism by both the Academy of Science and that of Medicine. The publication of his theory of animal magnetism in French in 1779, declaring that it was a scientific fact, created quite a sensation. The clergy immediately denounced him, attributing his many cures to the work of the devil. The medical establishment also denounced him as a fraud and a charlatan, as he was curing cases that they had deemed to be incurable.

Mesmer himself did not help matters with the authorities at all. He began dressing in long, lilac-colored magicians' robes, behaving in an eccentric manner, and openly verbally taunting his detractors at the French Academy of Medicine. That he was curing the ill that the Medical Faculty could not help was a well-known fact they could not dispute. In medicine, success in curing difficult cases is the surest route to condemnation by the established authorities.

Dr. Charles Deslon, a prominent member of the Paris Faculty of Medicine became one of Mesmer's first converts to his theories of animal magnetism. First serving as Mesmer's assistant, he eventually established his own clinic. Despite receiving Deslon's active support, the Paris Faculty of Medicine did not endorse Mesmer's work.

Mesmer soon found strong support among the nobility, including the patronage of the young Marquis de Lafayette. He then received a small pension from another aristocrat. This resulted in his opening a hospital where there were three "banquets" (or backquets) for magnetic healing, at one of which the poor were treated without charge. These banquets were tubs filled with magnetized rocks and other objects. They all had iron rods protruding from them. The person to be healed grasped one of these iron rods, and soon passed into a healing crisis, during which time they were often violent in their actions. After their crisis, they were quite often completely free from the condition that had previously afflicted them. Unfortunately the Mesmeric crisis, as it quickly became known, received a great deal of unfavorable publicity from both the always ready to condemn medical authorities and the prurient press, which then as now was far more interested in reporting horrors, shock, and scandal than informing the public of anything.

It is the rather disorderly scene of treatment at his hospital that is best known to us as Mesmer's magnetic cure. Mesmer himself took on some students, who also obtained similar cures. Accepting only those patients for treatment who had psychosomatic illnesses, and turning away those with real physical complaints, Mesmer and his associates treated and cured a great many psychosomatic conditions. Because of his recognized success with people who suffered from even the most severe psychological states, Dr. Mesmer is recognized today as the father of modern psychotherapy.

As Mesmer's fame grew, so did his eccentricity. He became involved with an oddly deviant, and somewhat openly occult, lodge of French Freemasonry. Further, he openly expressed several quite occult ideas in his treatment rooms. There, he was usually dressed in his magical robes as he walked among those being treated, carrying a wand, which he pointed at patients, or with which he touched them. His assistants dealt with those who were passing through more severe crisis, which Mesmer had associated with their healing. It was Mesmer's belief that to be healed, passing through an often violent and traumatic crisis was necessary.

In 1783, Mesmer founded a private academy to promote his ideas. This *Société de l'Harmonie* only lasted two years, as it was quickly wracked with dissension and internal argument. Mesmer would allow neither argument nor debate with what he believed were the great eternal truths that he had discovered. When some of his students, including the attorney Bergasse, the Marquis de Puysegur, and others, began making public some of the information Mesmer had revealed to them, Mesmer was publicly furious with them.

Although the majority of the people, most of the nobility, and the court, all favored Mesmer, King Louis XVI, who sat uncomfortably on the throne that was not to be his much longer, formed a royal commission in March 1784 to investigate the man who was now more popular in Paris than he. They approached Mesmer by investigating Dr. Deslon, who, as a member of the University of Paris Faculty of Medicine, was far more exposed to public criticism than Mesmer, the darling of the public. The members of the commission were chosen from among Mesmer and Deslon's known enemies at the Academies of Science and Medicine. They consisted of: the American ambassador, Benjamin Franklin as the chairman; Jean Bailly, the astronomer; Antoine Laurent Lavoisier, the chemist; Jussieu, the botanist; and the inventor of the instrument of execution which bears his name, Dr. Joseph Guillotine. Interestingly enough, in the aftermath of the French Revolution, King Louis XVI, Marie Antoinette, and all of the members of the committee but Franklin became victims of Dr. Guillotine's very sharp invention.

The royal committee attempted to replicate Mesmer's healing sessions. In several trials, lasting two and a half hours at a time, they sat around a container filled with magnetized rocks. These treatments failed to cure Franklin's gout, or any other known illness in those who were members of the committee. Dr. Deslon was taken to several trees in the garden of Franklin's Paris home. There he failed to identify the tree in which the committee had placed a magnet. As they could find no physical or logical basis for Mesmer's cures, the committee declared him a fraud, attributing his cures solely to the process of suggestion.

On August 11th, 1784, the members of the commission submitted their report to King Louis XVI. While they were forced to admit that Dr. Deslon had actually obtained cures, they said that there was no physical or sensible reason for these cures to have occurred. The cures that had been obtained were then ascribed to suggestion, and to the fertile imagination of the patients themselves. The French Academies of Science and Medicine had achieved their goal. Deslon's, and through him, Mesmer's, work was now condemned in Paris, just as Mesmer had previously been condemned in Austria. Mesmer left Paris in 1791, just as the violence of revolution overcame France. He went to Frauenfeld, a small village outside of Zurich, Switzerland where he lived peacefully for a time.

Sometime between 1798 and 1802, Mesmer returned to Paris, where he received compensation for the losses he had received due to the violence of the revolution. The compensation was enough money to keep him in moderate comfort for the rest of his life. In 1803, he was invited to return to Paris, but he respectfully declined. In 1812, Mesmer also declined the opportunity to go to Germany, although invited by both the King of Prussia and the Prussian Academy. He instead moved to Meersburg, a village near his birthplace, where he died peacefully on March 15th, 1815.

Mesmer and Hypnotism

Mesmer is frequently credited today with both the discovery and the initial application of hypnotism, although that phenomenon, first discovered among relatively few of Mesmer's patients, was actually uninvestigated, and not even recognized, by him.

Initially, hypnotic phenomena was both investigated and exploited by one of Mesmer's followers, the Marquis de Puysegur. He had noticed that some of Mesmer's patients, instead of passing through a traumatic healing crisis, as Mesmer expected, fell into a somnambulistic trance. This response fascinated the Marquis, who found it to often be as healing as the trauma through which Mesmer's other patients passed.

Puysegur investigated this, and found that he could place some of those people into a hypnotic trance without using either Mesmer's magnetic processes or other dramatic effects. Through questioning those whom he had placed into the trance state, Puysegur found that he could obtain information of various kinds, of which he did not believe that the people had any prior conscious knowledge. This discovery quickly led Puysegur to believe that he had found the key to unlocking mysterious arcane and occult secrets of all kinds.

In fact, the trance state we call hypnosis may also be induced by chanting, drumming, or ritualized dancing. Trances had been known and utilized in various guises by many primitive tribes for centuries; it was just something new on the European scene. Even the laying on of hands, under certain conditions, had been known to produce the same trance effect we now call hypnosis.

As with many men who have obtained a small key to something, the Marquis de Puysegur thought that the trance state was far more than it actually was. While he used this process in healing, he also thought that it was the key to the mysteries of the hidden (nonphysical) worlds. By the time Mesmer was denounced, Puysegur had already broken with him, and was off on his own. He was then working almost exclusively with this new discovery of his, which we now call hypnotism. When the violent wave of revolution swept through France, Puysegur swiftly fled to Germany, where his discovery of the trance state was well received in the far more progressive Prussian court.

The Marquis de Puysegur was the first person to use the term "mesmerism," which first appeared in English in 1802. The term, and its related verb, "mesmerize" (first appeared in English in 1829), have now entered the English language to describe the act and achievement of a particular mental state, that of someone who is internally completely focused on something outside of himself or herself. The term is no longer applied to hypnotism, which has now moved far beyond Puysegur's initial discovery of the trance state.

Animal Magnetism

The term "animal magnetism" was first used in the early years of the 18th century, when both magnetism and electricity were considered great novelties. As so often happens, a hidden or unknown force was being explained in terms of the latest so-called scientific discovery. One of the enduring reasons for a belief in animal magnetism is found in the sensible, real influence, or force, of the animal vital energy. Most people can detect this force in a healthy living being. It is the same nonphysical energy that is referred to as the universal life force, prana, Od, Vril, or Akashic force, and that is called by many other names in almost all cultures.

This force or energy can be demonstrated by cupping your hands about an inch apart with the palms facing each other. If you are alive, you will usually be able to sense "something" between your palms. How you interpret the sensation is up to you. The "something" is, in fact, the presence of the universal life force. When it feels strong, you are full of vital energy, when it feels weak, you are correspondingly lacking in vital energy. From this simple physical effect, the theory of animal magnetism slowly grew and expanded, sweeping aside all common-sense objections, and leaving scores of true believers in its wake. Mesmer was one of the most convinced of these true believers, although there were many others during his time.

This same experiment may also be performed between two people sitting opposite each other, one with their palms up and the other with their palms facing down above their partner's. In a short time, they will both feel what they can define as either a "magnetic" or an "electric" current flowing between their palms. It is actually neither magnetic nor electric, but if you choose to call it that, you may certainly do so, knowing that many others have also identified this feeling in that same manner. What is actually being sensed is the mutual impingement of the vital life force of the two people.

In the early years of the 20th century, Kilner, an electrician at a London hospital, demonstrated that a suggestion could be implanted into the human aura by the process of forming and implanting a focused thought with a disciplined mind. He decided that the force of the suggestion had the same effect, or at least a very similar effect, on the human aura as the magnetic energy from an electromagnet, with which he had formerly worked to modify the aura. Not enough real research has been done in this area to say anything truly substantial about the effect of either the magnetic force, or how it modifies the human aura. Kilner's work does form the basis for certain theoretical considerations that there may possibly be some unknown or as yet undiscovered connection between human thought and magnetic energy.

Animal magnetism was briefly credited with being the same force as that of a magnetic field—just as the insertion of a strongly-willed thought into the human aura was seen by Kilner to have about the same visible effect as a magnetic field on the human aura. The process of implanting a strongly-willed suggestion into a person is very much like the process of hypnosis. However, hypnosis, as it is practiced by physicians and other mental health professionals today, is not at all the same as the therapeutic work practiced in the 18th century by either the Marquis de Puysegur, or even much less, by Dr. Mesmer.

A. Bhattacharya, who wrote on magnetic healing among other things, recommended that a person attempting to transmit or receive thoughts hold a magnet in their right hand. Charles Cosimano, a proficient promoter of magnetic and other psychotronic and occult devices, designed a thought-transmitter helmet that uses a number of magnets around its circumference. These magnets supposedly act as amplifiers for the thoughts of the wearer to be transmitted to others. Whether or not there is anything real to this supposed connection between thought and magnetic energy is a valid question, but it is one that only serious and carefully designed research can ultimately answer. It is unlikely that anyone will undertake this research in the near future, as true and accurate ESP research is not a very popular academic field today.

None of these effects are really related to animal magnetism, which is only a name for the effect of the universal life force found in all living things, as it is seen operating between the extremities of one person, or between two or more people.

A dozen or so years ago, there was a brief flurry of interest in this kind research when it was discovered that different cultures have different comfort distances that they tend to stand at when they are communicating with each other in a one-on-one situation. Among other things, it was noticed that those who feel seriously threatened at a greater distance by people approaching them from the back are liable to be more violent than those who do not feel threatened until the distance between them is quite small. Some psychological research was done on this subject, but it was abandoned when it seemed to the researchers that all that could be discovered was judged to have been found.

Real animal magnetism, or to give it a proper name, the real effect of the conscious or subconscious projection of the life force, from one person to another, is accomplished through such hands-on therapies as finger pressure, acupuncture, shiatsu, massage, and other kinds of body work. In these therapies, the vital energy of the therapist passes into the body, as well as into the aura, of the person being treated. The trained therapist, using their contact healing system, supposedly has more of the vital energy, the life force, at their disposal than the person they are treating. Through their therapeutic efforts they are supposedly able to heal, or at least to make more comfortable, the person on whom they are working.

Unfortunately for Dr. Mesmer, this effect is a good long distance from his original therapeutic claims. Animal magnetism may well exist, but it is a property of the living animal, and it is not magnetic at all. As to whether it is influenced by the planets and the universe, we must reply with the "Scotch verdict," saying that this has not been proven.

Notes

1. Currently in print as *Lucretius Carus Titus, On the Nature of Things*, John Selby Watson, trans. (Amherst, NY: Prometheus Books, 1998).

2. Alexander Neckham, *De Naturis Rerum, Libri Duo, with the Poem of the Same Author, De Laudibus Divinae Sapientiae*, Thomas Wright, ed. (London: Longmans, 1863).

3. A collection of these "travelers lodestones" is located at the Museum of the History of Science, in Oxford, England.

4. Petrus Peregrinus de Maricourt, *Epistula de Magnete. Nova Compisitio astrolabii particularis* (Pisa, Italy: Scuola Normale di Pisa, 1995).

5. Robert Norman, *The Newe Attractive Variation of the Cumpas* (London: W. J. Johnson, 1974).

6. Gilbert's book was so well written that it has often been called the first truly scientific work written on any subject.

7. See note 14, where one such peer-reviewed study is mentioned.

8. There actually has been some research done on the effect of these devices. The results, as the saying goes, are quite mixed. The research that I have seen

does not tend to support the claims of those who sell these devices. However, it is an interesting experimental concept, and one probably worth investigating. While I would not purchase one of these usually expensive devices, making one for your personal experimental use is simple enough that it might be worthwhile.

9. Some occult and spiritual supply houses sell pre-matched paired lodestones. Unless you trust their ability to match lodestones, it is better to order two pairs, so that you can use the best matched pair of the two for your charm. Try to find out if they actually match the lodestones or just send two lodestones when you order a pair. The better supply houses actually take the time to match the stones, which increases their price quite a bit. For lodestone charms intended to bring about a marriage, the actual fit of the lodestones is quite important.

10. The Borderland Sciences Research Foundation publication, *Vitic, or Magnetic Vitality*, credits on page 1 *The Origin and Problems of Life* by A. E. Baines (London, Routledge & Sons, Ltd.; New York: E. P. Dutton & Co., 1921) as the source of this idea. I have been unable to locate a copy of this book.

11. *Vitic, or Magnetic Vitality*, p. 3. Brackets are my addition.

12. *Vitic, or Magnetic Vitality*, p. 2. Brackets are my addition.

13. The book was *Witness to Witchcraft* by Harry B. Wright, published by Funk and Wagnalls, New York in 1957. I recall the story well, as I have used it to illustrate this point several times in talks with others in the occult arts.

14. When having a physician friend of mine review this material, I was told of the following studies in the

healing effect of magnets. I have not read them, and doubt that I could appreciate them if I did. I place them here should you be interested in researching them: Carlos Valbona, M.D., Carlton F. Hazelwood, Ph.D., Gabor Jurida, M.D., "Response of pain to static magnetic fields in post polio patients: A double blind pilot study." Archives of Physical Med. Rehabilitation 1997; 78:1200-3; Dr. med. Thomas Laser, head physician of the orthopedics department, "Double blind study of the therapeutic effectiveness of permanently magnetized foils on secondary myotendofasciopathies at different selected locations". Klinic Bavaria, 8351 Schaufling. This does not seem to have been published in a peer-reviewed journal, as the journal is not cited.

15. Karla Gale, "Magnetic Field May Help Smokers Quit," Reuters, September 26, 2003.

16. "McLean Hospital Psychiatric Update," December 30, 1988, copyright © 2003, President and Fellows of Harvard College.

17. Matías A. Loewy, "Magnets Repair Birth Defect in Food Pipe," Reuters, September 26, 2003.

18. Walter Kilner's book, *The Human Aura*, was first published in London in 1920. It has been kept in print ever since, by a variety of publishers. Currently, it is published by Kessinger Publishing (January 2003) in paperback format. Kilner used colored screens and special glasses to view the various facets of the human aura.

Annotated Bibliography

Ancient Technology

The following references were supplied by Dr. Paul J. Gans, on his *Medieval Technology Pages* on the Internet: *http://scholar.chem.nyu.edu/tekpages/Technology.html*. Should you have a computer with Internet access, you should look at these pages to see just what our ancestors believed, and how they lived. They are all quite interesting.

Gies, Frances and Joseph Gies. *Cathedral Forge and Waterwheel: Technology and Invention in the Middle Ages*. New York: Harper Perennial, 1995.
Gimpel, Jean. *The Medieval Machine: The Industrial Revolution of the Middle Ages*. Baltimore: Penguin, 1976.
White Jr., Lynn. *Medieval Technology and Social Change*. New York: Oxford University Press, 1962.

Magnetic Devices

Magnetic Sleep Pads. Sales literature of MagnetiCo, Inc. 5421 11th Street, N.E. #109, Calgary, Alberta, T2E 6M4 Canada.

Vitic or Magnetic Vitality. Various authors. Eureka, CA: Borderland Sciences Research Foundation, 1990.

Walewski, Count Stefan Colonna. *A System of Caucasian Yoga.* Indian Hills, CO: Falcon's Wing Press, 1955.

History of Magnets

Eneas: A Twelfth Century French Romance. John A. Yunck, trans. New York: Columbia University Press, 1974.

Developing Clairvoyance with Magnets

Crystal Gazing and Clairvoyance. London: Nichols & Co., 1910.

Magnetic Energy Systems & Water De-scaling

Advertising material from The Magnetizer Group, Inc. of Gardenville, PA. This company, which sold magnetic devices for water de-scaling, is now out of business.

Magnetism—General Information

Lee, E. W. *Magnetism.* New York: Dover Publications, 1970.

Magic

Mathers, S. L. MacGregor. *The Book of the Sacred Magic of Abramelin the Mage.* New York: Dover, 1974.

————. *The Key of Solomon the King.* Escondido, CA: Book Tree, 1998.

Mickaharic, Draja. *A Century of Spells.* York Beach, ME: Weiser Books, 1985.

Yronwode, Catherine. *Hoodoo Herb and Root Magic.* Forestville, CA: Lucky Mojo Curio Co., 2002.

Magnetism—Biological Effects

Baines, A. E. *The Origin and Problems of Life.* London: Routledge & Sons, Ltd.; New York: E. P. Dutton & Co., 1921.

Bloch, George, trans. *Mesmerism: A Translation of the Original Scientific and Medical Writings of Dr. F. A. Mesmer.* Los Altos, CA: William Kaufmann, 1980.

Burke, Abbott George. *Magnetic Therapy.* Oklahoma City: Saint George Press, 1980.

Cerney, J. V., D.P.M. *Handbook of Unusual and Unorthodox Healing Methods.* West Nyack, NY: Parker Publishing Company, 1976.

Davis, Albert Roy and A. K. Bhattacharya. *Magnets and Magnetic Fields or Healing By Magnets.* Calcutta: Firma KLM Private Limited, 1970.

Davis, Albert Roy and Walter C. Rawls, Jr. *The Magnetic Effect.* Smithtown, NY: Exposition Press, 1974.

————. *Magnetism and Its Effects on the Living System.* Smithtown, NY: Exposition Press, 1975.

Holzapfel, E., P. Crepon, and C. Philippe. *Magnet Therapy.* Translated from the French. London and New York: Thorsons Publishing Group, 1981.

Lawrence, Ron, M.D., Ph.D., Paul J. Rosch, M.D., FACP, and Judith Plowden. *Magnet Therapy: The Pain Cure Alternative.* Rocklin, CA: Prima Publishing, 1998.

Payne, Buryl. *The Body Magnetic.* Santa Cruz, CA: Buryl Payne, 1988.

Whitaker, Julian, M.D. and Barbara Adderly, M.H.A. *The Pain Relief Breakthrough.* New York: Little, Brown and Company, 1998.

Dr. Franz Anton Mesmer

Buranelli, Vincent. *The Wizard from Vienna: Franz Anton Mesmer.* New York: Coward, McCann & Geoghegan, 1975.

Fishbough, William. *Library of Mesmerism and Psychology.* New York: Fowler and Walls, 1852.

Gauld, A. Alan. *A History of Hypnotism,* Cambridge, England: Cambridge University Press, 1995.

Goldsmith, Margaret. *Franz Anton Mesmer: The History of an Idea.* London: Arthur Barker, Ltd., 1932.

Wycoff, James. *Franz Anton Mesmer: Between God and the Devil.* Englewood Cliffs, NJ: Prentice Hall, 1975.

Occult Devices

Cosimano, Charles. *Psionics 101.* St. Paul, MN: Llewellyn Publications, 1987. This book deals with psychotronic devices, only a very few of which are magnetic in nature.

Index